Ghana

Ghana

BY ETTAGALE BLAUER
AND JASON LAURÉ

Enchantment of the World™
Second Series

Children's Press®

An Imprint of Scholastic Inc.

NEW YORK   TORONTO   LONDON   AUCKLAND   SYDNEY
MEXICO CITY   NEW DELHI   HONG KONG
DANBURY, CONNECTICUT

Frontispiece: Women carry containers near Kumasi

Consultant: Naaborko Sackeyfio, Assistant Professor of History, Dartmouth College, Hanover, New Hampshire

Please note: All statistics are as up-to-date as possible at the time of publication.

Book production by Herman Adler

Library of Congress Cataloging-in-Publication Data

Blauer, Ettagale.
  Ghana / by Ettagale Blauer and Jason Lauré.
    p. cm. — (Enchantment of the world. Second series)
  Includes bibliographical references and index.
  ISBN-13: 978-0-531-20652-2
  ISBN-10: 0-531-20652-1
  1. Ghana—Juvenile literature. I. Lauré, Jason. II. Title. III. Series.
  DT510.B56 2010
  966.7—dc22   2009006656

© 2010 by Scholastic Inc.
All rights reserved. Published in 2010 by Children's Press, an imprint of Scholastic Inc.
Published simultaneously in Canada.
Printed in China.

SCHOLASTIC, CHILDREN'S PRESS, and associated logos are trademarks and/or registered trademarks of Scholastic Inc.
1 2 3 4 5 6 7 8 9 10 R 19 18 17 16 15 14 13 12 11 10   62

Ghana

Cover photo:
Ghanaian woman

Contents

CHAPTER

 ONE Connecting Past and Present........................ 8

 TWO The Lay of the Land............................. 14

 THREE A Look at Nature................................. 26

 FOUR Ghana Through Time 36

 FIVE Governing Ghana 58

 SIX A Growing Economy............................ 66

 SEVEN The People of Ghana.............................. 78

EIGHT The Spiritual World............................. 86

NINE Rhythms of Life 94

TEN A Day in the Life................................110

Volta River

Timeline **128**

Fast Facts **130**

To Find Out More **134**

Index **136**

Meet the Authors **142**

Goldweight

Connecting Past and Present

GHANA IS A VIBRANT NATION IN WEST AFRICA, A crossroads of cultures. In 1957, Ghana became the first African nation to gain independence. Prior to that, it was a colony of Great Britain. In 2007, the people of Ghana celebrated a half century as a nation. The life of one man, Rikki Wemega-Kwawu, who was born two years after Ghana gained independence, captures the history of the nation and celebrates its achievements.

Opposite: **A woman sells bananas and other produce at a market in rural Ghana.**

Ghanaian teenagers participate in an event celebrating the 50th anniversary of Ghanaian independence.

Wemega-Kwawu was born in Takoradi, a city along the coast. "From the time I was a child," he says, "I was interested in art. In Ghana, people did not recognize this as a career. Everyone wants you to become a doctor. My mother was a teacher, and my father was a mechanical engineer. He wanted me to become an engineer."

Wemega-Kwawu's schooling reflects Ghana's modern history. He went to St. Augustine's College, a Catholic school. At school, he spoke English, and at home, he spoke two other languages, Fante and Ewe. In 1998, his artistic skill earned him a spot in a summer course in the United States, at the Skowhegan School of Painting and Sculpture in Maine.

Rikki Wemega-Kwawu poses with one of his artworks made from phone cards.

In order to talk to his family back in Ghana, he began buying phone cards. With these cards, he could make long-distance calls at low rates. As an artist, he had worked in pastels, oil, and acrylic paints, but, he says, "The first card I saw, I thought it was so beautiful. I thought I would make a work of art. I started collecting them." The result was an artwork he called *Kente for the Space Age*. Kente is the name of a type of cloth that was once reserved for the Asante kings of Ghana. Members of Wemega-Kwawu's own family wove kente cloth. "I recognized the cards as fabric," he says.

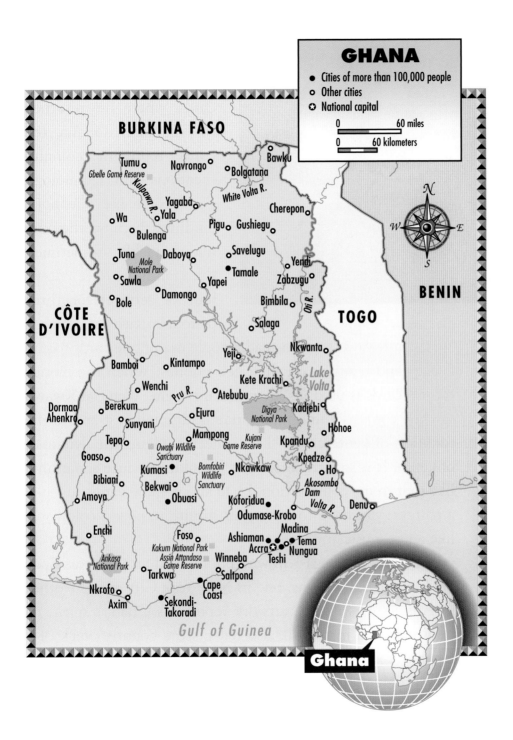

GHANA

- Cities of more than 100,000 people
- ○ Other cities
- ✪ National capital

0   60 miles

0   60 kilometers

BURKINA FASO

Tumu
Gbelle Game Reserve
Navrongo
Bolgatana
Bawku
Kulpawn R.
White Volta R.
Yagaba
Yala
Cherepon
Wa
Pigu
Gushiegu
Bulenga
Savelugu
Tuna
Daboya
Yendi
Mole National Park
Tamale
Zabzugu
Sawla
Yapei
Bole
Damongo
Bimbila
Oti R.
Salaga
BENIN
CÔTE D'IVOIRE
TOGO
Nkwanta
Bamboi
Kintampo
Yeji
Lake Volta
Wenchi
Kete Krachi
Pru R.
Atebubu
Kadjebi
Dormaa Ahenkro
Berekum
Ejura
Digya National Park
Hohoe
Sunyani
Mampong
Kujani Game Reserve
Kpandu
Tepa
Owabi Wildlife Sanctuary
Kpedze
Goaso
Bomfobiri Wildlife Sanctuary
Nkawkaw
Ho
Kumasi
Bibiani
Bekwai
Amoya
Obuasi
Koforidua
Akosombo Dam
Denu
Odumase-Krobo
Volta R.
Enchi
Madina
Foso
Ashiaman
Tema
Kakum National Park
Accra
Nungua
Assin Attandaso Game Reserve
Winneba
Teshi
Ankasa National Park
Tarkwa
Saltpond
Nkrofo
Cape Coast
Axim
Sekondi-Takoradi
Gulf of Guinea

N
W   E
S

Ghana

In Ghana, people are much more likely to use cell phones than telephone landlines.

Wemega-Kwawu continued to collect phone cards when he returned to Ghana. In Ghana, the cards represent communications and technology. Few people use telephone landlines because they are undependable. "Sometimes, the landlines are down [out of service] for three or four months at a time," Wemega-Kwawu says. Instead, people use phone cards to call friends and relatives on their cell phones. When the money on the cards is used up, they discard them. Wemega-Kwawu saw the cards as a link to Ghana's traditional past and to the tradition of kente cloth. "I have been studying the dynamics of kente. It is so jazzy. I thought I could introduce something like that in my composition. I had about 4,000 cards. Just like a painter, you have to trust your intuition, pick a color; just like a jazz musician."

In 2008, Wemega-Kwawu's phone-card artwork was honored in two exhibitions, one in New York City and the other in Austria. His unique artwork represents Ghana's spirit, its traditions and history. It also reflects the country's lack of a reliable communications system and its inventive way around that problem. In his phone-card art, he has captured the essence of modern Ghana.

Communication and technology are at the heart of Ghana's leap into 21st-century employment. In Accra, the capital city, U.S. insurance companies and other businesses have established many call centers where skilled, English-speaking people answer calls from customers. The people in Ghana answer questions about insurance policies from people in the United States.

The call centers are made possible by a satellite link that allows information to be sent instantaneously. This link is part of a new, international fiber-optic network that flows around the African continent. As such technological improvements bring new opportunities to young Ghanaians, artists like Rikki Wemega-Kwawu will continue to bridge the gap between traditional Ghanaian society and the modern world.

Workers process U.S. health insurance data at an office in Accra.

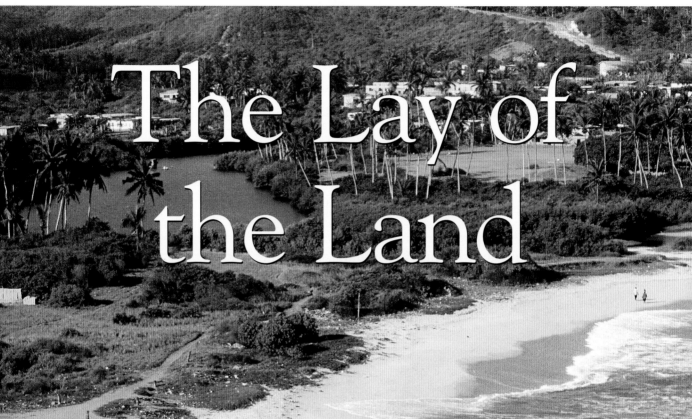

C H A P T E R

T W O

The Lay of
the Land

14

The city of Cape Coast lies on hills overlooking the Gulf of Guinea.

THE NATION OF GHANA IS LOCATED IN WEST AFRICA along the Gulf of Guinea, a part of the Atlantic Ocean. Ghana covers an area of 92,456 square miles (239,460 square kilometers), nearly the size of the U.S. state of Oregon. It is shaped like a rectangle, with the short sides forming the northern and southern borders.

Ghana shares its land borders with three countries. To the west lies Côte d'Ivoire, to the east is Togo, and to the north is Burkina Faso. The waters of the Gulf of Guinea lap against Ghana's shoreline in the south.

Opposite: **Fishing boats line a beach in Abanze, along the central coast.**

Ghana's Geographical Features

Area: 92,456 square miles (239,460 sq km)

Largest Artificial Lake: Lake Volta, about 250 miles (400 km) long

Largest Natural Lake: Lake Bosumtwi, 19 square miles (49 sq km)

Highest Elevation: 2,887 feet (880 m), Mount Afadjato

Lowest Elevation: Sea level, along the Atlantic Ocean

Coastline: 335 miles (539 km)

Average High Temperatures: In Accra, 88°F (31°C) in January and 81°F (27°C) in July

Average Low Temperature: In Accra, 73°F (23°C) in both January and July

Average Annual Precipitation: In Accra, 32 inches (81 cm)

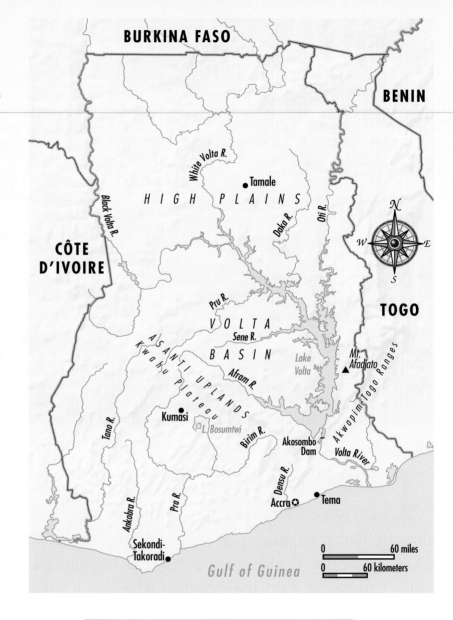

Land Regions

Most of Ghana is made up of flat plains and small, rolling hills. The country is divided into five geographical regions: coastal plains, tropical forests, the Akwapim-Togo Ranges, the Volta Basin, and high plains.

Plains border the coast in the south of the country. The coast is a mix of sandy beaches and saltwater lagoons. Moving eastward along the coast, away from the capital city of Accra, the land slopes upward, gradually forming small ridges and rounded valleys. These gentle hills are well suited for farming, though low-lying areas become swampy during the rainy seasons. The changing wetlands make travel in this region very tricky. Boats must make their way around unmarked channels and sandbars that change shape as the water rises and recedes. In addition, the cold, rough surf of the Atlantic Ocean routinely pounds the coast, making shipping treacherous. Ghana, despite its long coastline, has no natural harbors. Artificial harbors have been built at Takoradi and Tema.

Takoradi Port, in the twin cities of Sekondi-Takoradi, is the largest port in Ghana.

North of the coastal plains lie tropical forests, which cover about one-third of Ghana's total area. This forested region is divided into two subregions, the Asante Uplands and the Kwahu Plateau. Much rain falls in this region, so farmers are able to grow thirsty cash crops such as cocoa and coffee. People also grow plantains, yams, and cocoyams, a starchy root, to feed themselves.

The rugged Akwapim-Togo Ranges lie along the country's eastern border. This region is home to Ghana's highest point, Mount Afadjato, which rises to 2,887 feet (880 meters).

In Ghana's tropical forests, tall trees tower above a thick tangle of low-growing plants and vines.

Dry grassland and sparse trees blanket northern Ghana. From December to March, strong winds blow down from the desert to the north, producing especially hot days.

The Volta Basin takes up most of central Ghana. The great Volta River runs through this region. The Volta Basin has poor soil, and farmers who live there struggle to make a living.

High plains dominate the northern third of the country. Much of the high plains and the Volta Basin is savanna, a type of grassland with few trees. This is the driest part of Ghana. In the north, brief rainy seasons are followed by extremely dry seasons during which no rain falls at all. The region's scattered trees store water in their trunks and roots during the rainy seasons. They draw on this moisture in the dry months. This dry north has the sparsest population in the country.

Looking at Ghana's Cities

Accra, Ghana's capital, is the largest city in the nation. The second-largest city is Kumasi, which lies on Lake Bosumtwi about 100 miles (160 km) north of the Gulf of Guinea. Nearly 1 million people live in the beautiful, green, hilly city. Kumasi is the center of Ghana's gold-mining region and is in a major cocoa-growing area. It is the principal city of the Asante people. The city was founded by the Asante king Asantehene Osei Tutu in 1695. Today, the Asante king lives in Kumasi's Manhyia Palace. People shop in the vast open-air Kejetia Market (right), the largest such market in West Africa. The Centre for National Culture in Kumasi includes a museum of Asante history, a library, a crafts shop, and an exhibition hall.

Tamale, the third-largest city in Ghana, lies in the dry northern part of the country. It is home to about

300,000 people, most of whom belong to the Mole-Dagbon ethnic group. Tamale is the commercial center of northern Ghana and one of the fastest-growing cities in West Africa. It has become a gateway for travel to Burkina Faso, Togo, Côte d'Ivoire, and other countries in the region.

The twin cities of Sekondi and Takoradi combine to form the fourth-largest city in Ghana, with a total population of about 270,000. The cities lie on the coast about halfway between Accra and the border with Côte d'Ivoire. Takoradi, originally a fishing village, was chosen to be Ghana's first ocean port in 1928. Since then, it has grown into the country's largest port (left). Sekondi has been an important naval base since colonial times.

Tema is a rapidly growing port city. Development generated by the construction of Akosombo Dam, to the north, has seen Tema's population grow from about 35,000 in the early 1960s to more than 250,000 today. Tema's commercial port adjoins a lively fishing port.

Ghana's major river is the Volta River. It is actually two rivers. Both begin their journey in the neighboring country of Burkina Faso and head southward to the Gulf of Guinea. The White Volta travels through the center of Ghana, and the Black Volta runs along Ghana's western border and then turns eastward until it meets up with the White Volta.

A canoe makes its way up the Volta River, the largest river in Ghana.

The southern part of Ghana is also laced with other rivers, including the Pra, the Tano, the Ankobra, the Birim, and the Densu. Some are seasonal—they flow when the rains fall, then slowly dry up and wait for the next rainy season. Others flow year-round, fed by water trickling down hillsides. The drier northern region of the country has fewer dependable rivers, making it difficult for people to live there. Ghana's population is concentrated in the south, where water is plentiful.

The Agumatsa River flows through the mountains near the Togo border. It thunders over a cliff to form the Wli Falls, the highest falls in West Africa.

Lake Volta, Ghana's most prominent geographic feature, is one of the largest artificial lakes in the world. The lake was created in the 1960s when Akosombo Dam was built on the Volta River. This unusual body of water sprawls along the eastern part of the country, with branches that look like wide rivers reaching far into the center of the country. The lake is about 325 miles (520 km) long and has an average width of 16 miles (26 km). The size and depth of the lake vary with the seasonal rains. Just after the rainy season, the lake achieves its greatest depth and covers the biggest area, roughly 3,700 square miles (9,500 sq km).

A ship travels over Lake Volta, which cuts across southeastern Ghana.

Akosombo Dam

In 1915, a British engineer named Albert Kitson first dreamed of building Akosombo Dam. He had learned that the Kwahu Plateau held a large deposit of bauxite, a mineral used to make aluminum. He wanted to use electric power from the dam to process the bauxite, but the colonial government felt building a dam would be too expensive.

When Ghana won its independence from Great Britain in 1957, President Kwame Nkrumah ordered that the dam be built. Construction began in 1961, and the dam was completed in 1966. Building the dam employed tens of thousands of Ghanaians but caused much disruption. Before the lands were flooded by the new lake, 84,000 people living in 740 small communities had to be relocated. The people lost their ancestral lands, where they and their families had lived for generations.

The great wall that forms Akosombo Dam and holds back the waters of Lake Volta stands 374 feet (114 m) high and measures 2,165 feet (660 m) across. In most years, the dam produces enough electricity to supply all of Ghana and the nearby countries of Togo and Benin.

Ghana is warm year-round, with an average annual temperature of about 80 degrees Fahrenheit (27 degrees Celsius). The south of the country is often damp and humid, while the north is drier. In the north, dusty winds called the harmattan blow sands south from the Sahara between November and March.

Some parts of Ghana receive as much as 83 inches (211 centimeters) of rain a year, while others receive less than 40 inches (100 cm). The country has distinct rainy and dry seasons. These seasons vary from region to region. In much of the country, there are two rainy seasons, one from March to July and the other from September to November. Some areas have shorter rainy seasons. The interior has only one rainy season, but it stretches from April or May to October.

A young Ghanaian takes shelter during a downpour.

A Look
at Nature

A band of baboons walk down a dirt road in Mole National Park in northern Ghana. Baboons live in habitats ranging from grasslands to forests.

Vast forests once covered the southern half of Ghana. But in the mid-20th century, the government allowed logging companies to harvest valuable timber from large tracts of land. Many animals were also poached, or hunted illegally. Since then, a number of areas have been set aside as national parks to protect the land and the remaining wildlife.

Opposite: The rare bongo antelope lives in reserves in Ghana.

A Look at Nature **27**

Elephants have a drink at a waterhole in northern Ghana. An adult elephant drinks about 60 gallons (225 liters) of water a day.

Large animals such as elephants and lions were once common across the savanna. Today, they are mostly found in national parks and reserves. Other animals such as chimpanzees, leopards, bongo antelope, duikers, and crocodiles also live in Ghana, mostly in reserves.

Snakes are found throughout Ghana, and some of them are very dangerous. Two of the most dangerous snakes are the cobra and the black mamba. There are also pythons and puff adders.

More than 725 bird species have been spotted in Ghana. They include parrots, kingfishers, eagles, herons, and egrets.

The black mamba is fast and aggressive. It kills its prey with a quick bite.

Many kinds of fish live in the waters off of Ghana's coast. Species include herring, bonitos, flying fish, tuna, mackerel, and sole. Barracuda and stingrays are also found in the ocean waters.

Farmers in Ghana see some wildlife not as a national treasure but as a nuisance. Elephants sometimes wander out of the game reserves and eat farmers' crops.

Barracudas grow up to 6 feet (1.8 m) long. They use their strong teeth to snatch prey.

Visiting the Treetops

Ghanaians have turned Kakum National Park into the highlight of their national reserve system. The park is located 12 miles (20 km) north of the city of Cape Coast, on the central coast. More than 100,000 people visit the park each year to view its varied wildlife. Kakum is home to forest elephants, a different species than the elephants found on the plains of East Africa. It is also home to antelope, monkeys, and more than 200 species of birds and butterflies.

The best way to see a dense tropical rain forest is from above. The highlight of a visit to Kakum is the aerial walkway, called the skywalk. It is the only such walkway in Africa. The narrow skywalk is 1,093 feet (333 m) long and hangs 88 feet (27 m) above the ground, suspended from eight enormous trees.

The rain-forest vegetation is thick, and it wraps around itself to form a canopy, a kind of umbrella of treetops. Visitors to Kakum cautiously follow the skywalk, high above the forest floor. Wooden platforms attached to the eight anchoring trees allow visitors to stop and observe the forest life around them from the height of a 12-story building. They get a true bird's-eye view of the forest canopy, where many birds and other species live.

The Upside-Down Tree

The baobab tree is sometimes called the upside-down tree because of its odd appearance. It has a huge, thick trunk that grows very tall. Then, from the top of the trunk, thin branches sprout that look more like roots than branches. The baobab has no leaves most of the year.

The kinds of trees and other plants that grow in Ghana vary greatly from region to region, depending on the climate. Along the coast, the plants are mainly tall grass and a kind of low growth called scrub. Plants form clumps around termite mounds, which are sometimes 10 feet (3 meters) tall. The savanna is mainly grassland. Some trees, such as baobabs, acacias, and shea trees, grow amid the savanna grassland.

Termites create mounds that contain chambers and a maze of tunnels. Millions of termites live in a large mound.

Common trees in Ghana's southern forests include the silk cotton tree, the wawa tree, and the African mahogany. Forests once covered about 30,000 square miles (80,000 sq km), but timber companies and farmers have reduced this amount dramatically. In some regions, as much as 90 percent of the forest cover is gone. When forests disappear, the soil cannot hold as much water. It dries up, and the climate becomes hotter and drier.

A truck hauls away huge logs in Ghana. Logging, farming, and industry have destroyed the vast majority of Ghana's forests.

The government of Ghana is trying to reverse the loss of the forest by requiring that loggers replant trees. The Ministry of Lands, Forestry and Mines has also created a program to plant more than 346,000 acres (140,000 hectares) of forest in an effort to keep Ghana green.

Digging mines often destroys forests. Some mining companies are now planting trees to grow new forests on mining sites.

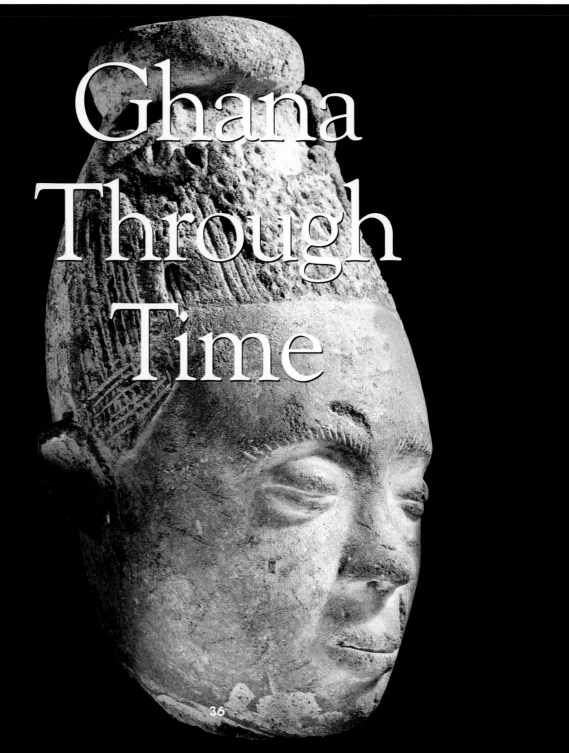

Ghana Through Time

The history of ancient Ghana can be read through the evidence left behind by the earliest people. Scientists and historians have determined that people were living in the region of Ghana as long as 6,000 years ago. Ghana's early people made their homes in the lush forests. The area's many rivers and streams provided rich fishing.

Opposite: **An Asante sculpture of a head**

Settling in Ghana

Some archaeologists—people who study the remains of past societies—believe that the Asante people may have come to

The Asante people lived in thatched-roof huts positioned around a central courtyard.

The Kingdom of Ghana

Long before Ghana became a nation, there was a different place called Ghana. The kingdom of Ghana, founded by the Soninke people, was located north of present-day Ghana, where the countries of Mauritania and Mali are today.

Much of what we know about this kingdom was recorded by al-Ya'qubi, an Arab writer of the 9th century CE. He described the kingdom in detail, writing about its rulers and their magnificent treasures of gold.

Ghanaian rulers wore gold bracelets that were so heavy they could not lift their arms. Gold threads were woven into their fabrics. The kingdom's people were great hunters and warriors who also controlled the gold trade.

Although the wealthy kingdom of Ghana died out in the 11th century, people remembered it. When the colony the British called the Gold Coast gained its independence from Great Britain in 1957, it called itself Ghana.

the Ghana region 2,000 years ago. The Asante cultivated the land, growing vegetables and grains including yams, plantains, onions, and millet.

Through the years, people continued to move into the area from the north and the east. The presence of gold in Ghana, along with the introduction of new food crops into the region, set the stage for larger, permanent populations to form. The Akan-speaking people, who today live in the southern part of the country, established themselves at the end of the 15th century. At the same time, the Mande people took control of the northern half of Ghana, along with the region that would become Burkina Faso. The Mande were active in trading kola nuts and gold for cloth and metal. The Mande were Muslims, followers of the religion of Islam.

The Asante Gain Control

The Asante had the most influential early kingdom in Ghana. They were active in trade, supplying gold, ivory, and enslaved

An Asante horseman equipped for war. The Asante were the most powerful group in early Ghana.

people to Europeans. The Ga, Fante, and other coastal peoples served as middlemen. The Asante had a well-organized society, with a system of chiefs who controlled groups of families. The Asante formed a large army and gained control of neighboring groups. By the end of the 17th century, Asante leader Nana Osei Tutu became "Asantehene," or king of the Asante. He organized all the Asante groups and conquered other groups such as the Akyem, creating an empire with a capital at Kumasi. During his reign, Asante kings began using the Golden Stool as a symbol of their power.

The Asante empire expanded until it came into contact with other southern peoples: the Fante, the Ga, and the Ewe. The Ewe and Ga were fishermen who traded fish for agricultural products. The Fante and the Ga moved into Ewe territory to escape the Asante. In time, the Ga and the Fante adopted some Ewe customs.

Goldweights

Gold figured so prominently in Asante trade that the people devised a system of measures to weigh the gold dust. These brass figures, called goldweights, were used on balance scales. Each merchant had a set. Many different patterns and images were depicted on goldweights. They showed living creatures, mythical beings, or objects from daily life. A knot design sometimes used on goldweights was a symbol of wisdom, representing leadership and the king. Porcupine shapes were also popular because their fierce quills represented the strength of Asante warriors.

The Golden Stool

During the reign of Asante king Nana Osei Tutu, a priest who advised Tutu created the legend of the Golden Stool. Among the Akan and the Ga peoples, a stool is a symbol of power. It is used not as a seat but to show that a royal person is in command. According to the story, the priest brought down from the sky a wooden stool covered in gold. It floated down to earth and came to rest on the lap of Osei Tutu. The priest then declared that the soul of the Asante nation lived in that stool. It became the most sacred object in the Asante kingdom.

A new Asantehene, or Asante king, takes power in a ceremony called an enstoolment. He does not sit on the Golden Stool. Instead, he is raised and lowered over the stool three times, never touching it. The Golden Stool is removed from its safe place only on special occasions. It remains a powerful symbol of the Asantehene and all the Asante people.

The Portuguese were the first Europeans to arrive on the African coast. In 1471, the first Portuguese arrived on shores that are now part of Ghana. The Portuguese king rewarded the seafarers for each length of coast they acquired. They were given the exclusive right to trade in that land.

Wherever they landed, the Portuguese built sturdy forts and castles, many of which still stand today. The first castle, built in 1482, was named St. George of the Mine Castle, and is known now as Elmina Castle. The name Elmina is taken from Portuguese words that mean "the mine." The Portuguese

The Portuguese built Elmina Castle in 1482. They transported all the materials used to build the fort to Ghana aboard 10 ships.

lived in the forts and castles and established trade agreements with the Africans. Later, the Portuguese used the forts as defenses against other Europeans who wanted to take over the same territory.

The Portuguese came to the region to trade for gold. When they arrived along Ghana's coast, they named it the Gold Coast. They saw gold glittering in the streams. The mines of the Gold Coast produced as much as 30,000 ounces (850,000 grams) a year for the Portuguese king.

Gradually, trade in enslaved people replaced trade in gold. For nearly a century, the Portuguese had no competition along the Gold Coast. They made deals with the local chiefs, who provided them with enslaved people. Sometimes, the Portuguese captured slaves on their own.

A slave auction room at Elmina Castle. In some years, 30,000 enslaved people passed through Elmina before being transported to the Americas.

Slavery

The institution of slavery began in ancient times and developed in societies around the world. In Africa, it was established as early as the 10th century. Africans who had been captured in the region of present-day Sudan, in northeast Africa, were taken across the Sahara and sold. Most were women who were used mainly as servants and farmworkers. Other Africans were shipped north, to the Mediterranean, where they were sold as servants or laborers to Spain, Portugal, and other European countries.

Slavery existed in the Gold Coast before the first Europeans arrived there in 1471. People captured during wars in the Gold Coast became unpaid laborers for the victors, but they were always regarded as human beings. It was European traders who first saw slaves as trade goods rather than as people. They shipped enslaved Africans across the Atlantic Ocean in chains, packed tightly together. Many enslaved people died during the crossing.

Some Ghanaians traded Africans to Europeans for guns and cloth. With guns, Ghanaians could defend themselves against attacks from other groups. The chiefs grew more powerful and captured more people to be sold as slaves.

No one knows for sure how many people were sold and shipped out of Africa. It is estimated that 10 million Africans were sold into slavery. Experts believe that at least half a million people were sold and shipped away from the Gold Coast alone. The picture above is a recreation from a film about the slave trade.

Making Connections

Each year, many Americans visit Ghana. The country is a particularly important destination for African Americans. In their brief visits, they see the buildings, now known as slave forts, where slaves were held in captivity before they were sent on their long, treacherous journey out of Africa. They search the faces of the Ghanaians, hoping to make a personal connection. For one African American, that connection was realized.

Maya Angelou is a well-known author and poet. When she went to Ghana in 1962, she struggled to find her place in the country as an African and an American. She searched for some connection between her 20th-century self and her 18th-century ancestors. And then, one day, she found that connection in a small town called Keta. The slave trade had hit the Ewe village very hard. Virtually all the adults were taken away. Children watched as their parents were put into chains, never to be seen again.

Those children grew up in the homes of people who lived nearby. Through the generations, the story of how they lost their parents was told over and over again. Suddenly, into their little town there came a woman

who looked just like them but who said she was from America. She was living proof that at least some of their ancestors had survived.

Maya Angelou left Ghana glad to be alive, glad that her ancestors had survived the dreadful trip across the ocean. She tells this story in her book *All God's Children Need Traveling Shoes.*

The trade was challenged by the Dutch, who were also great sailors. In 1637, Elmina Castle fell to the Dutch, and by 1642, the Portuguese had lost their grip on the Gold Coast. Throughout the rest of the 1600s and the 1700s, a variety of Europeans made landfall along the coast and made trade deals with the Africans. By 1872, the British had fought off all other contenders, becoming the major power on the Gold Coast.

A Colony Takes Shape

The Asante were the most powerful group in the interior of the region. Starting in 1807, the Asante invaded and attacked the southern coastal area. They wanted to take control of the trade that had developed in gold, timber, and palm oil. They successfully attacked the coastal forts, forcing the Europeans to sign a treaty. This agreement extended Asante rule over these coastal regions. The Fante and the Ga had relied on the British for protection, but the British were unable to protect them from the Asante. The British made treaties with coastal chiefs who wanted to use the power of the British against the Asante.

Kumasi, a city in what is now south-central Ghana, served as the Asante capital.

In 1843, the British government named Commander H. Worsley Hill the first governor of the Gold Coast, and a colony began to take shape. The Gold Coast was a British protectorate, which meant that the British governed it using local chiefs, rather than taking full control of the territory. In 1872, the Dutch sold Elmina Castle to the British, ending the Asante's trading outlet to the sea.

Meanwhile, the Fante people formed an independent confederation. This confederation, near Accra, was modeled on the European nations and was viewed with alarm by the British. If the Africans could organize themselves as the Europeans had, the British could not use their governing ability as an excuse to stay in power. In 1874, Britain declared the confederation illegal and made the Gold Coast a colony.

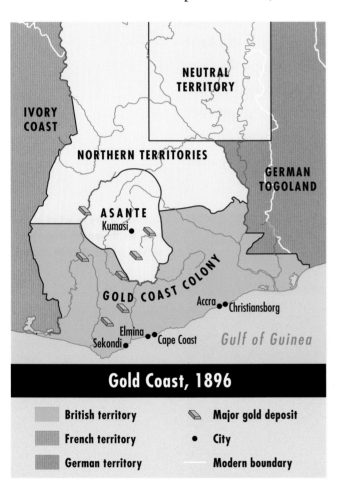

Gold Coast, 1896

British territory	Major gold deposit
French territory	City
German territory	Modern boundary

Asante Resistance

The Asante had a well-established culture and system of chiefs and kings, which helped them resist British rule. Kumasi, the Asante capital, was a well-organized, sophisticated city. Traders wishing to come into the region passed through a series of tollgates.

There were vast markets where customers could find goods from many parts of the world. The Asante army was huge, estimated at 200,000 men. Skirmishes between the British and the Asante occurred periodically throughout the 19th century. When the British invaded in January 1874 to force the Asante to agree to British control, they came in force.

The British were at a tremendous disadvantage in the Gold Coast. Not only did the Asante have huge numbers of men ready to fight, but they were also used to the extremely hot and humid climate. The British had to march through the wilderness loaded down with gear. They also had to face an enemy they could scarcely see: mosquitoes infected with malaria, a disease that could be spread with a single bite. Malaria killed many people in Africa, and it left others too weak to stand or walk.

British troops fire on Asante soldiers in late 1873. The following year, the British took official control of the Gold Coast.

The British, however, had superior weapons. The fire-power of their rifles and cannons was overwhelming. They conquered Kumasi and declared themselves victors, but they needed to find the Asante leader so he could sign the peace treaty. While they were waiting, the British stripped the city of everything of value that they could carry away. Much of it was made of gold. When they had everything they wanted, they set fire to Kumasi, destroying it. The British victory weakened the Asante kingdom. At the same time, a civil war within the kingdom threatened to destroy the entire Asante culture.

In 1896, the Asante finally became part of the British protectorate. The British ended the position of Asantehene

Dividing Africa

In 1884, German leader Otto von Bismarck asked the representatives of 14 major European powers to meet in Berlin, Germany, to talk about their claims to parts of Africa. At the conference, European nations made deals dividing Africa among themselves. The idea was to avoid conflicts over territory. By the end of the conference, Great Britain, France, Portugal, and Germany had each claimed huge parts of Africa. Belgium's King Leopold claimed the Congo region as his own personal territory.

and sent the Asantehene who was then in power, Prempeh I, into exile. In 1901, the British proclaimed the region of Asante a colony, to be ruled by the governor of the Gold Coast. The British had explored regions beyond the land of the Asante and now claimed those territories as well.

The British did not allow Prempeh I to return to Kumasi until 1924. By this time, the British felt that the Asantehene would not challenge their authority. He died in Kumasi in 1931. In 1935, a new Asantehene was named, Nana Osei Agyeman Prempeh. For the first time since 1896, the carefully guarded Golden Stool was displayed in public.

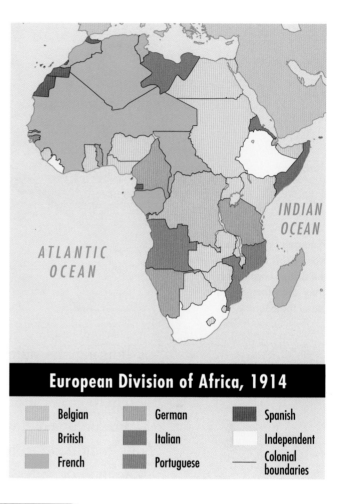

European Division of Africa, 1914

Belgian	German	Spanish
British	Italian	Independent
French	Portuguese	Colonial boundaries

Governing the Colony

By now, the three territories of the Gold Coast—the coast itself, Asante, and the dry, sparsely populated Northern Territories—were united under British rule as the Gold Coast. The British also ruled many other colonies in Africa.

In the Gold Coast, the British used a system called indirect rule, in which they relied on traditional chiefs to rule their own people. This reduced conflicts with the British. But

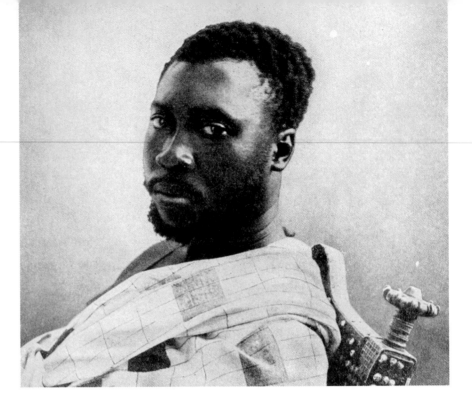

Prempeh I ruled the Asante from 1888 until 1896, when the British captured him. They soon forced him to leave the country.

by limiting the number of people who took part in making decisions about their own lives, they did not allow a political system to grow naturally.

Britain urged development in the Gold Coast. The British built a railroad connecting coastal cities. They also built thousands of miles of roads. They increased production of cacao, used to make chocolate. Cacao became a great source of income for the colony. Much economic progress was made under Frederick Gordon Guggisberg, governor of the Gold Coast from 1919 to 1927. He worked to provide clean water, sanitation, energy, and other services.

During the early years of the colony, schooling was made more widely available. Secondary schools and a teachers' training college opened. In 1948, University College began admitting students.

As these changes were taking place, the people of the Gold Coast began to think of themselves as members of distinct nations, but not the kinds of nations designed by the Europeans. People in Africa wanted to direct their own destinies.

During the 1930s and 1940s, Great Britain ruled both the Gold Coast and India. During World War II, the British urged the Africans in their colonies to help them fight in Asia. There, African soldiers met Indian soldiers who were fighting on the side of the British. The Indians were also struggling for their own independence. The Africans began to wonder why they were fighting for Britain instead of for themselves. In 1947, India gained its independence, and the British could see that they were going to have to start a process leading to independence for the Gold Coast, too.

The Path to Independence

When the soldiers returned to the Gold Coast, they began fighting for their independence in a movement led by Kwame Nkrumah. He traveled around the country, talking to people, convincing them that the time was right for them to have their freedom. He urged his people to practice civil disobedience, a peaceful way to fight against unfair laws.

In 1949, Nkrumah helped establish the Convention Peoples' Party (CPP), Ghana's first important political party. As movement for independence gained strength in Ghana, the British responded by arresting Nkrumah. While Nkrumah was in prison, Komla Gbedema, vice chairman of the CPP, took his place at rallies. He carried around a full-sized photograph of Nkrumah. He would prop this up at all the meetings, saying, "Nkrumah's body is in jail but his spirit is going on."

In 1951, Britain allowed free elections for a national assembly. Though still in prison, Nkrumah and the CPP won by a landslide. Nkrumah was named prime minister. The British had no choice but to release Nkrumah from prison.

On March 6, 1957, the Gold Coast became the independent country of Ghana. It was the first black African colony to achieve self-rule, to become a nation. U.S. vice president Richard Nixon and civil rights leader Martin Luther King Jr. attended the ceremony. Ghana's independence inspired many other people across Africa to seek independence from their colonial rulers. It was seen as the beginning of a new era across the continent.

Cadets stand at attention as the flag of Ghana is raised over the parliament building during the ceremony making Ghana independent.

The First President

Kwame Nkrumah, Ghana's first president, was born in 1909 in the village of Nkroful. He attended a mission school, where he was singled out as an outstanding student. This earned him a place at a teachers' training college in Accra.

After teaching for several years, he went to the United States, where he earned degrees from Lincoln University in Pennsylvania and the University of Pennsylvania. He spent 10 years in the United States, forming the political ideas that brought him back home to Ghana in 1947. By this time, he was a strong supporter of Pan-Africanism, a movement that encouraged Africans to unify to achieve their goals. When he founded the Convention People's Party in 1949, his goals were to achieve independence and democracy for the Gold Coast and to help others in West Africa achieve independence.

Nkrumah became Ghana's first president in 1957, and he soon forced his views and policies on the

nation. By 1966, Ghanaians were angry at his rule, and the army took over the government while Nkrumah was away. He lived the rest of his life in the West African country of Guinea, where he died in 1972.

Nkrumah's Rule

Nkrumah believed that political freedom was just the first step for Ghana. He also wanted the country to have economic freedom. He invented a system of central planning that he called "scientific socialism." He tried to keep control of every aspect of life in Ghana. He controlled the amount of money farmers earned for their crops, which contributed to food shortages. He planned huge projects, like a hydroelectric plant, but used all the money in the country's treasury to pay for the plant.

After Kwame Nkrumah was forced from power, some Ghanaians knocked over a larger statue of him that had stood in front of Accra's central police headquarters.

Nkrumah also took tremendous power for himself. He changed the constitution so that only his followers would be in charge of government departments. He manipulated elections to be sure they would be decided in his favor. Afterward, he declared that he was backed by the will of the people. He had opponents jailed. One important opposition leader, Kofi Abrefa Busia, fled to London when Nkrumah declared Busia's United Party to be illegal.

When Nkrumah had gained power, he declared himself president for life. Nkrumah made himself the symbol of the country. His picture appeared on everything from women's dresses to the nation's coins. At the same time, the government established a network of spies. People could not say anything negative about Nkrumah without facing arrest.

During his rule, Nkrumah weakened the power of the traditional chiefs and removed some of them from power. This broke a tradition that stretched back a thousand years. Although Ghana had a strong economy based on its exports of gold and cacao, Nkrumah spent money extravagantly on the Akosombo Dam, aluminum production, and other projects. Overspending, combined with corruption and low prices for the country's resources, used up the country's cash reserves. He was forced to borrow money to pay for basic goods.

Nkrumah knew that the country's only university, at Legon, near Accra, could not admit all the students who wanted a college education. But the country needed educated people. He began a major plan to upgrade existing schools into universities and to build new schools, including the University of Cape Coast.

Despite such positive steps, many people opposed his rule. On February 24, 1966, while Nkrumah was out of the county, the Ghanaian military overthrew his government. Barely nine years after he led the country to independence, Nkrumah fled Ghana, leaving behind shattered hopes and an economy in ruins.

Kofi Busia worked as a college professor before entering politics.

New Leaders

As soon as Nkrumah was overthrown, opposition leaders were released from prison, and Kofi Busia returned to Ghana. The new government faced overwhelming odds. It had to get the economy back on its feet and foster the people's trust in the government. This proved to be nearly impossible. In 1969, Busia was elected prime minister. With the debts left behind by Nkrumah, his efforts to get the economy back on track were doomed. On January 13, 1972, the military overthrew Busia.

Jerry Rawlings held power in Ghana for two decades.

Rawlings's Rule

For most of the time from 1972 until 1993, Ghana was under military rule, which meant that no one elected the leaders. Now, military leaders were fighting for control. In 1979, Jerry Rawlings took over the government by force. He stepped aside, letting a civilian government under Hilla Limann take over. But then, on December 31, 1981, Rawlings overthrew Limann. He held military power until 1992, when he permitted elections to be held. Rawlings was elected president, but opposition parties claimed that the elections had not been fair. They refused to take part in elections to parliament. As a result Rawlings's party easily took over the 200-seat parliament. He was reelected in 1996.

During his rule, Rawlings tightened control over the press. He shut down an independent radio station and seized its equipment. In 1998, two newspaper editors, Harruna Atta and Kweku Baako, were jailed for a month for criticizing Rawlings's wife.

A Democratic Transition

In spite of his violent history and dictatorial rule, Rawlings obeyed Ghana's two-term limit on the presidency. In December 2000, Ghana enjoyed the first democratic presidential change of power in its history. John A. Kufuor of the New Patriotic Party (NPP) defeated John Atta Mills, who had served as Rawlings's vice president. Eight years later, in December 2008, Mills was elected president with 50.23 percent of the vote. It was the closest election in Ghanaian history.

Such peaceful and democratic changes of government are a major milestone in Ghana's growth as an independent nation. Like many countries, Ghana went through some tough growing pains. Today, it seems headed for a future in which the citizens can trust their government and have faith in their president. This is a huge achievement for a young nation.

John Atta Mills (far left) took office as president in January 2009.

Governing Ghana

58

G HANA IS A REPUBLIC, A NATION IN WHICH THE PEOPLE elect their leaders. The nation's constitution, which was enacted in 1992, divides the government into three branches: executive, legislative, and judicial.

Opposite: **A woman casts her vote in the Ghanaian presidential election in December 2008.**

The Executive Branch

The head of the executive branch is the president, who serves as both head of government and chief of state. The president is elected by the people to a four-year term and is limited to two terms. The president must be Ghanaian by birth and at least 40 years old.

The president appoints a vice president and a council of ministers, who advise the president in different areas such as foreign affairs, health, and finance.

The National Flag

Ghana's flag has three horizontal stripes of red, gold, and green. In the center of the gold stripe is a black five-pointed star. The green represents the country's forests, the red stands for the blood of those who died fighting for independence, and the gold represents the country's mineral wealth. These are the traditional colors of liberation in Africa. The star stands for African freedom, and it stands alone because Ghana was the first black African country to become independent.

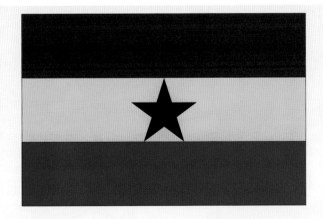

A council of state also advises the president. It has 25 members. Eleven are nominated by the president, 10 are elected from the regions, and 4 represent Ghanaian institutions such as the National House of Chiefs. All Ghanaians at least 18 years old are eligible to vote.

Ghana was ruled by the military for much of its history, but today it has just 5,000 people in the armed services. This number represents the smallest proportion of military service people in the population of any country in the world.

Officials meet in the Ghanaian parliament in 2003.

The Legislative Branch

The Parliament is Ghana's lawmaking body. It has 230 members who are elected for four-year terms. Members debate proposed laws and usually vote along political party lines, with the party in power generally winning. A Ghanaian must be at least 21 years old to be elected to Parliament.

The Judicial Branch

Ghana's legal system is based on the constitution,

A lawyer (far left) and a politician talk outside a court in Accra.

Ghanaian common law, and traditional laws. Common law is rooted in the British system of laws, and traditional laws are based on the customs of the various ethnic groups in the country. Many traditional laws govern the distribution of land and inheritance rights.

The Supreme Court is the highest court in the land. It reviews decisions made in other courts and determines whether laws follow the constitution. Below the Supreme Court at the national level are the Court of Appeal and the High Court. District courts, traditional courts, and local courts apply laws at the local level.

NATIONAL GOVERNMENT OF GHANA

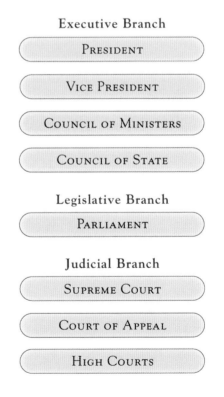

Executive Branch

PRESIDENT

VICE PRESIDENT

COUNCIL OF MINISTERS

COUNCIL OF STATE

Legislative Branch

PARLIAMENT

Judicial Branch

SUPREME COURT

COURT OF APPEAL

HIGH COURTS

The National Anthem

Ghana first adopted the song "God Bless Our Homeland Ghana" as its national anthem in 1957. The lyrics have since changed twice. The current lyrics were adopted in 1966.

God Bless our homeland Ghana

And make our nation great and strong

Bold to defend for ever the cause of Freedom
and of Right.

Fill our hearts with true humility

Make us cherish fearless honesty

and help us to resist oppressor's rule

With all our will and might for evermore.

Hail to thy name, O Ghana.

To thee we make our solemn vow;

Steadfast to build together

A nation strong in Unity

With our gifts of mind and strength of arm

Whether night or day, in mist or storm

In every need whate'er the call may be

To serve thee, Ghana, now and evermore.

Raise high the flag of Ghana

And one with Africa advance

Black Star of hope and honor

to all who thirst for liberty

Where the banner freely flies

May the way to freedom truly lie

Arise, arise, O sons of Ghanaland

And under God march on for evermore.

Local Government

Ghana is divided into 10 administrative regions. To carry out the laws, each region is divided into 110 districts. Each district is subdivided into town councils, zone councils, and so on, until they reach the level of unit committees. This brings some form of law to every person in the country.

Local governments are responsible for the development of their towns and villages. They decide on ways to raise funds through taxes. The councils organize yearly meetings of the people under their rule to discuss economic development.

The Role of Chiefs

Ghana tries to honor the ways different ethnic groups governed themselves in the past. A system of chiefs, for example, governed communities for centuries, long before Ghana became a nation. Local chiefs continue to guide the lives of people in rural areas of Ghana. The chiefs interpret and apply traditional laws that have a day-to-day impact on the people in their area. When a dispute arises, the people involved discuss the problem thoroughly with the chief. Because of this, when the chief makes a decision, people will consider it fair.

Senior members of a community choose the new chief. The position is usually passed down through a family, although not always to the eldest son. Sometimes, for example, a brother of the chief might be considered a better choice. Among most ethnic groups in Ghana, the symbol of the chief's position is a stool, and the ceremony in which he becomes the chief is called enstoolment. In parts of northern Ghana, however, a skin represents the position of the chief. After becoming chief, a person begins using the title *Nana*, which means "grandfather" or "ancestor."

The leader of the Fante chiefs wearing traditional clothing. Chiefs retain power in many parts of Ghana.

Accra: Did You Know This?

Accra is a big city that is home to 1.7 million people, but it still has the feeling of the small town it once was. The name Accra comes from *nkran*, an Akan word for the black ants that are found in the area. Accra is located on the coast and enjoys a warm but humid climate. Temperatures rarely vary more than a few degrees, with the daily high temperature usually around 86°F (30°C).

Before independence, Accra had served as a capital since 1877, when Ghana was still the Gold Coast. Government and business offices are spread throughout the city. The city's major sites include the National Theatre, Independence Square, and the Kwame Nkrumah Mausoleum [below]. The National Museum features displays showing the country's heritage, including royal stools, kente cloth, Asante gold weights,

wooden carvings, and drums. Exhibits also show how some crafts are made. The Arts Centre (above) is the largest craft market in Accra. Makola Market is the major market for household goods and is well known for its selection of beads and fabrics. The Obruni Wa Wu Market specializes in used clothing, most of it donated by foreigners and shipped to Ghana to be sold.

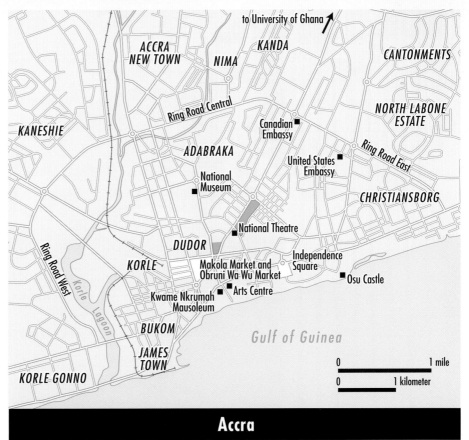

Accra

A Growing Economy

GHANA'S ECONOMY HAS LONG BEEN DOMINATED BY ONE mineral, gold; one crop, cacao; and one natural resource, timber. In the 1990s, the country started moving into the modern communications age. Computers were introduced to a small number of people. At the same time, Internet cafés started to spring up and people began using cell phones. These technological changes helped open up new job opportunities for the people of Ghana. Modern technology creates jobs for computer technicians, data-processing clerks, and cell phone salespeople. There are new international call centers in Accra.

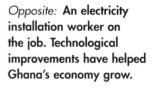

Opposite: **An electricity installation worker on the job. Technological improvements have helped Ghana's economy grow.**

Ghanaians work at computers at a busy Internet café in Accra.

A Growing Economy **67**

Rich stands of forest once covered most of the southwestern part of the country, from the border with Côte d'Ivoire east to Accra. Much of this forest has been cleared for farmland. About half the working population of Ghana is employed in agriculture, either by growing food for family use or by working on large-scale farms. Cacao, which is used to make chocolate,

The Story of Cacao

Cacao beans are turned into cocoa paste, the basic ingredient of chocolate. The bean is quite bitter before it is processed. Ghana is one of the largest producers of cacao beans in the world, usually ranking second in production. When conditions are right, Ghana can produce 385,000 tons (350,000 metric tons) of cacao beans in the growing season.

There are two stories about how cacao came to Ghana. According to one story, it began in 1878, when a Ghanaian returning to Ghana brought the first cacao pods into the country. Another story declares that cacao was brought into the country by Swiss missionaries after they had tried unsuccessfully to grow tea. Either way, under British rule of the Gold Coast colony, planting was carried out on a large scale. Ghana became a one-crop country, totally dependent on the income from cacao but at the mercy of bad weather and the production of competing countries. By the end of the 1940s, the country was producing half of the world's cocoa.

is grown across the middle of the country, south of the Black Volta River. It is a cash crop, which means that it is sold outside the country to earn money for the growers. Most of the cacao is grown on small plots measuring less than 7 acres (3 ha) each. Many thousands of Ghanaians work on the cacao farms, where the pods containing cacao beans grow on small trees.

Manufacturing

Clothing, timber products, aluminum, iron, and steel are all manufactured in Ghana. Food processing is also an important part of the economy. Much of the cacao grown in Ghana is processed in the country. In 2008, the country processed 275,000 tons (250,000 metric tons) of cacao.

Many women in northern Ghana gather shea nuts and process them into rich shea butter. This is used to make high-quality soaps and creams, much of which are exported to Japan. In one workshop in Tamale, the women have formed an association of shea-butter producers. Together, they produce more than 22 tons (20 metric tons) of shea butter a month.

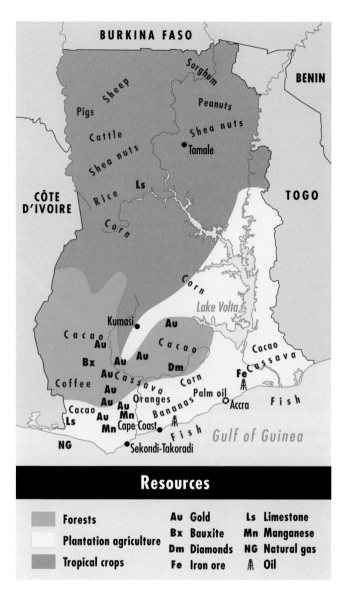

Resources

Forests	Au	Gold	Ls	Limestone
Plantation agriculture	Bx	Bauxite	Mn	Manganese
	Dm	Diamonds	NG	Natural gas
Tropical crops	Fe	Iron ore	⚒	Oil

A worker drills into a wall at the Obuasi gold mine. Gold has been mined on the site since the 1600s.

Mining

Miners have been removing gold from beneath Ghana for hundreds of years. Yet much gold remains, and Ghana is one of the world's leading gold producers. The country produced about 133,000 pounds (60,000 kilograms) of gold in 2004. There are two basic methods of gold mining. One method is to sink a shaft into the earth, send miners down to blast out the ore, and then bring the ore to the surface for processing. The other is to reach the ore by shaving off layers of the earth's surface. This is called opencast, or open-pit, mining. Both types of mining are used at the Obuasi gold mine in the Asante region. It is the largest opencast gold mine in Africa.

A Culture of Gold

Gold has long been a vital part of the Asante culture. Women traditionally panned for gold in streams, while men dug pits from which gold-bearing ore was taken. Special gold objects were made for members of the royal family.

Gold is a soft metal that can be worked with simple hand tools. Ghanaians make gold objects by hammering the gold into very thin sheets, or by drawing it into extremely fine wire. Gold became the basic element of trade in the region of Ghana in the 16th century. In return, chiefs were given glass beads made in Venice, Italy. They became known as trading beads because they were also traded for enslaved people.

Ghana also has other mineral deposits, including bauxite, manganese, and iron ore. It has two working diamond deposits, at the Brim and Bonza diamond fields. About 1 million carats of diamonds are unearthed annually at Brim and Bonza. The diamonds found there are not as valuable as the gem diamonds used for jewelry. Instead, they are used in the manufacture of other products.

What Ghana Grows, Makes, and Mines	
Agriculture	
Cacao (2005)	736,000 metric tons
Coffee (2006)	790,000 metric tons
Manufacturing	
Textiles (2005)	39 million yards
Timber products (exports, 2005)	466,155 cubic meters
Mining (2006)	
Gold	66,205 kilograms
Diamonds	973,000 carats
Manganese	1,600,000 metric tons

Timber

Logging companies have been harvesting timber from Ghana's vast stretch of forested land since the early 20th century. Today, logging remains important to the economy. In 2008, Ghana exported about US$170 million worth of wood. But this income has a high price. Each year, about 1.7 percent of Ghana's forests are destroyed. Illegal logging also takes a huge toll. Many people cut down trees and then burn them to create charcoal to use for cooking fuel.

A sawmill in Kumasi. Wood products are an important part of Ghana's economy.

Fishers push their boat out into the Gulf of Guinea. Anchovies and round sardinella are the most common catch in Ghana.

Fishing

The waters off the Ghanaian coast offer rich fishing. Fishers also bring in many tons of fish from Lake Volta. They go out in handmade dugout canoes along the lake's long shoreline. About 124,000 Ghanaians feed their families by fishing. Fante fishers sometimes travel along the African coast, ranging as far away as Senegal to the northwest and Cameroon to the southeast seeking fish.

After the fish are caught, Ghanaian women salt, dry, or smoke them to preserve them. Ghanaian women work along the shore, processing and marketing fish, but only men are permitted in the fishing canoes.

Three major companies can much of the tuna that fishers bring ashore at Tema. In one year, Ghana exports tuna worth US$50 million.

Technicians test blood samples in Ghana. Health care is an important service industry.

Services

Much of the fish caught in Ghana is sold at local markets. This selling is part of the service sector of the economy. In the service sector, people do things for others, rather than making or growing a product. Teachers and salespeople, bus drivers and doctors all work in service industries.

A growing service industry in Ghana is international customer service. Some U.S. businesses hire English-speaking Ghanaians to answer calls from their customers. Thousands of new jobs have been created in Accra, employing college-educated men and women. In a high-rise building called the Pyramid, hundreds of people work at computers, reading health-insurance claims for the U.S. insurance company Aetna. When a worker in Ghana has filled in the necessary information, the form is sent back to the United States. It costs Aetna about one-tenth the price to employ a worker in Ghana than to have the same job done in the United States.

Tourism is a growing service industry in Ghana. People come from around the world to visit the country's national parks, tour Elmina Castle, and relax on the beach. This creates thousands of jobs for people who work in hotels and restaurants and for guides and taxi drivers. In 2006, 442,000 tourists visited Ghana, spending US$345 million.

The service sector also includes shipping and transportation. Although Ghana's long coastline does not have any natural harbors for large ships, large ships dock at the artificial harbors of Tema and Takoradi. The Port of Tema now handles 80 percent of the cargo entering and leaving Ghana. The main exported products are manganese, bauxite, cocoa, and timber. The main imports include oil and wheat.

Tema is the busiest port in Ghana.

Taking the Tro-Tro

The *tro-tro* is a common form of public transportation in Ghana. It is a minivan that follows a particular route around town or between towns. A tro-tro usually seats 12 to 16 people, but often more people climb onboard. Unlike traditional buses, the tro-tro has no established stops. It will pick up and drop off people anywhere along the route. Because the tro-tro makes so many stops, it can sometimes take a long time to go short distances.

Money Facts

The official unit of currency in Ghana is the cedi, pronounced "C-D." One cedi contains 100 pesewas. Over the years, the value of the cedi declined so much that it might cost 1,000 cedis to ride on a tro-tro. Because the cedi was worth so little, bills were issued in huge denominations, and people carried enormous amounts of cedi notes with them in order to buy ordinary goods such as food and clothing.

Then, in 2007, the Ghanaian government revalued the currency. The old 10,000-cedi note was replaced with a 1-cedi note. The new bills were issued in banknotes valued at 1, 5, 10, 20, and 50 cedis. Coins were issued in amounts ranging from 1 pesewa to 1 cedi. The front of the new bills depicts a group of prominent political figures along with Accra's independence arch.

The back of the bills features important structures, such as Akosombo Dam and the Balme Library at the University of Ghana. In early 2009, US$1 was equal to 1.34 new cedis.

Energy

Ghana's major source of electricity is Akosombo Dam, on the Volta River. The water pouring through the dam spins turbines that generate electricity. Water accumulates in Lake Volta during the rainy seasons between July and November. During dry periods, there is sometimes not enough water going over the dam. This creates a shortage of electricity. When this occurs, the government sometimes has to limit the amount of electricity people can use.

In many parts of Ghana, people do not have access to electricity. But in Accra, people rely on electricity in their homes and businesses. When the power goes out, information on computers may be lost, small businesses may have to cut back on their employees' hours, and factories cannot produce goods. The biggest electricity consumer in Ghana is a company called Valco Aluminum. In a typical year, it uses 45 percent of all the electricity produced in the nation. From time to time, Valco has been forced to close because of power shortages.

Ghana is seeking new sources of electricity so these shortages will not happen. In 1997, a power plant that runs on oil went into operation at Takoradi. Although oil is expensive, it is readily available. Ghana is also looking into solar power, taking advantage of the tremendous amount of sunshine the country enjoys. Solar-powered street lamps at the University of Ghana provided power during one of Ghana's droughts, allowing students to study at night.

Ghana has begun to invest in solar power. Solar lights are now used on the University of Ghana campus.

People in villages need power to pump clean water. They need power to run refrigerators that keep medicines fresh. And they need lights so they can read at night. This electricity can be produced by solar panels at low cost. In the village of Timber Nkwanta, some people cook with solar power instead of firewood. The use of solar power leads to cleaner air, is less expensive, and will help preserve Ghana's dwindling forests.

The People of Ghana

MANY DIFFERENT ETHNIC GROUPS COMBINE TO FORM Ghana's rich culture. The Akan group, which includes the Asante and the Fante, is the largest. Its members live mainly in the south-central part of the country. The Mole-Dagbon live in the north, and the Ewe live in the east. The Ga people live in the coastal region.

In 2007, about 22.3 million people lived in Ghana. The population is very young, with children under 15 making up 38 percent of the total. Only 3.6 percent of Ghana's people are older than 65.

Opposite: **A young Fante woman in Cape Coast**

Who Lives in Ghana?

Akan (Asante and Fante)	49.3%
Mole-Dagbon	15.2%
Ewe	11.7%
Ga	7.3%
Guan	4%
Gurma	3.6%
Gurunsi	2.6%
Mande-Busanga	1%
Other	5.3%

A group of children in Accra

The People of Ghana **79**

Twi is one of the most common Akan languages. Here are a few Twi phrases:

Wo ho te sen?	How are you?
Me ho ye.	I'm fine.
Mepa wok yew	Please
Meda ase	Thank you
Aane	Yes
Dabi	No

Language

When the European powers divided up Africa among themselves, they insisted on the use of their own languages. Because of this, Ghana became an English-speaking country surrounded by three French-speaking countries: Côte d'Ivoire, Burkina Faso, and Togo. Any person from the Gold Coast who wanted to play a role in the development of the country had to learn to speak English. Using a common language helped tie the diverse peoples of the region together. Those in the more remote northern part of the country did not have much contact with English speakers and remain more isolated to this day. English is the official language of Ghana. In the cities, most people speak it.

Seventy-two distinct languages are spoken within the borders of Ghana. These languages break down into two major language groups—Kwa, which is spoken by the Akan and the Ewe, who live south of the Volta River, and Gur, spoken by people living north of the Volta River. Many Ghanaians speak several languages. Many people living in Accra learn to speak Ga, the local language. Ewe is a common language in the Volta region.

Naming Children

People who speak an Akan language often name their children according to the day of the week the child was born. In the Fante language, starting with Sunday, boys are named Kwesi, Kwadwo, Kwabena, Kweku, Yaw, Kofi, and Kwame. This tells you that former United Nations secretary-general Kofi Annan was born on Friday, and that Kwame Nkrumah, the first president of Ghana, was born on Saturday. Names for girls, starting on Sunday, are Esi, Adwoa, Abena, Akua, Yaa, Afua, and Amma.

In Legon, a wealthy suburb of Accra, two-story houses sit amid green lawns and decorative trees.

City Life

In recent years, many people have moved from the countryside to the cities. In 1970, just 29 percent of the population lived in urban areas. By 2007, 44 percent of Ghanaians lived in cities. Concrete blocks of apartments have been erected on the outskirts of Accra to house the rapidly expanding population. The city cannot keep up with the need for housing. Most people live on the outskirts in makeshift houses made of mud, corrugated iron, wood, and any material their owners can find. Middle-class homes, where most government workers live, are usually made of concrete with corrugated metal roofs. Two-story houses, including buildings that date from the colonial period with wide porches and beautiful gardens, line the roads in wealthy residential areas.

In cities, most people keep a few chickens or a pig in their yards. Even close to the heart of Accra, chickens cluck and pigs oink.

Population of Ghana's Largest Cities

Accra	1,700,000
Kumasi	650,000
Tamale	280,000
Sekondi-Takoradi	270,000

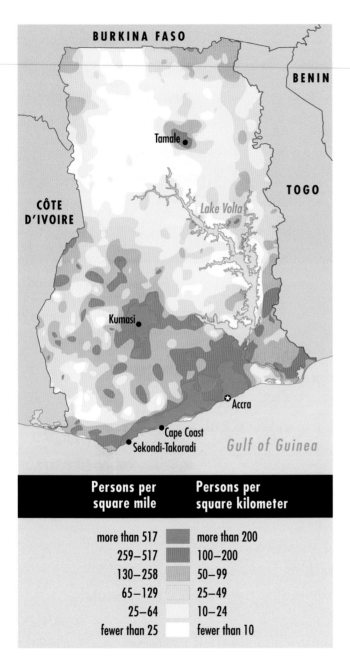

Persons per square mile		Persons per square kilometer
more than 517		more than 200
259–517		100–200
130–258		50–99
65–129		25–49
25–64		10–24
fewer than 25		fewer than 10

In the countryside, where most Ghanaians live, people spend much of the day doing household chores. Women walk great distances to get water for cooking and washing. They carry huge cans on their heads back to their homes. They pound root vegetables to use in cooking and cook over wood fires. They also walk great distances to gather firewood. Men and women tend their farms, where they grow vegetables. When people in the villages have problems or disputes, they turn to their local chiefs.

In the northern countryside, women build their own houses. The walls are made of mud that is often combined with a binding material such as straw or pieces of plants. Dried mud, called adobe, blocks the heat of the sun, creating a cool place to live, which is a big advantage in a tropical climate. Although the mud needs frequent repair, it is easily available— and it costs nothing.

In the Navrongo Saboro area, in the northern part of the country, women decorate their mud houses in beautiful geometric patterns. They make their own paints using natural materials. Each woman invents her own design and draws it on the wall, using grasses as a brush or applying the color directly with her fingers. The patterns are taken from traditional designs, but they are combined in original ways. Some women draw patterns directly into the mud before it dries, turning the entire house into a sculpture. Some patterns imitate the rows of kernels on an ear of corn, a daily food.

Many houses in other regions also have mud walls and tin roofs. Other people have houses made of cement blocks.

In some parts of northern Ghana, women decorate their houses with bold geometric designs.

The government of Ghana is determined to provide a good education for children. In primary school, children are usually taught in their first language for the first three grades. Then they learn English and other classes are taught in English. Children also study math, science, social studies, agriculture, and physical education.

Primary and middle school was made free and mandatory for all children in 1974. But parents must pay for books, supplies, and school uniforms. Because of these expenses,

Students work on their lessons at a school in Accra. Primary school begins at age six and continues for six years.

Kofi Annan

Prominent Ghanaian Kofi Annan (1938–) is a soft-spoken man who served as secretary-general of the United Nations (UN) from 1997 to 2007. Most of the world's nations belong to the UN, an organization devoted to peacefully solving conflicts between nations. People look to the head of the UN, the secretary-general, as the chief problem solver.

Annan is the son of a Fante hereditary chief. He grew up near Kumasi but spent most of his adult life outside Ghana. He attended Macalester College in Minnesota, where he received an undergraduate degree in economics. He later earned a master's degree from the Massachusetts Institute of Technology. Except for a brief period as managing director of the Ghana Tourist Development Company, he spent his entire career at the UN. Following his service there, Annan was appointed chancellor of the University of Ghana. He is also chairman of the Alliance for a Green Revolution in Africa. Established in 2006, the group's

mission is to help small-scale farmers and their families lift themselves out of poverty by improving farm productivity. Annan speaks several African languages as well as English and French.

parents cannot always afford to send their children to school. Some children do not attend school because they live too far away from the closest one. Today, about 75 percent of adult Ghanaians can read and write.

The University of Ghana is the country's leading university. It was founded in 1948, before Ghana was an independent nation. Nearly 30,000 students attend the university, studying subjects such as medicine, nursing, dentistry, agriculture, arts, geology, zoology, and languages.

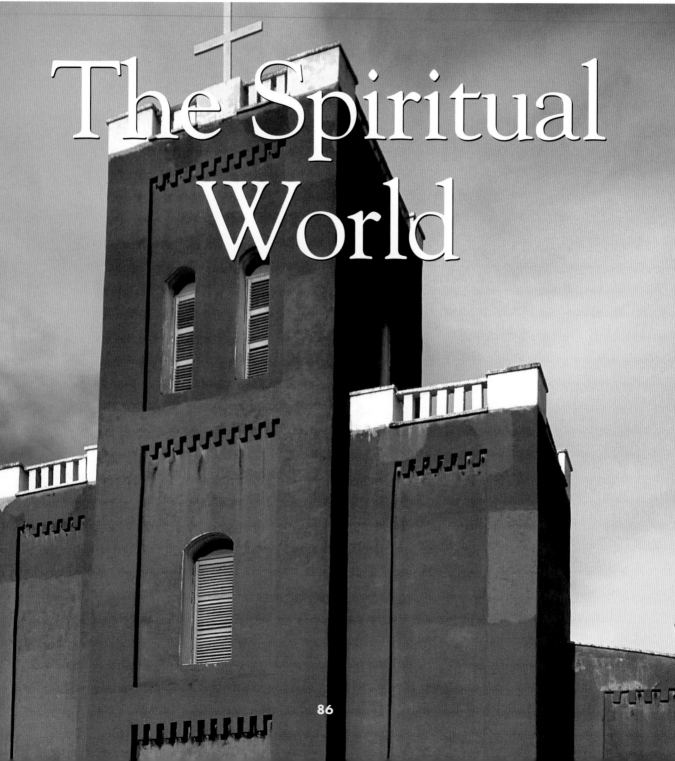

C H A P T E R
EIGHT

The Spiritual
World

86

THE PEOPLE OF GHANA PRACTICE A VARIETY OF RELIGIONS. In general, most people in the southern part of the country are Christian, whereas northerners tend to be Muslim. Many people throughout Ghana who practice Christianity or who identify themselves as Christians also keep their traditional beliefs. They combine the two religious belief systems and adjust the mixture to suit their needs.

Opposite: **Construction began on Navrongo Cathedral in 1906. Its walls are made of mud.**

Evangelical Christians worship at a church in Accra.

Religions in Ghana

Pentecostal/ Charismatic	24%
Protestant	18.6%
Islam	16%
Catholic	15%
Other Christian	11%
Traditional religions	8.5%
None	6.1%
Other	0.7%

Christianity

Christian missionaries have been active in Ghana since the Portuguese arrived in the region in the 15th century. Christianity became a strong presence in Ghana during the 19th century, when Presbyterian and Methodist missionaries arrived to try to convert local people to their religion. They established schools to attract people they wished to convert. At mission schools, Ghanaians could get an education, but they had to accept the religion of the mission.

Today, many different types of Christianity are actively practiced in Ghana. The largest groups are Pentecostals and Catholics. There are also Methodists, Anglicans, Mennonites, Presbyterians, Evangelical Presbyterians, and Baptists.

Ghanaians attend a Bible class at a church in Accra.

The mosque in Larabanga is the oldest Muslim house of worship in Ghana. It dates to the 13th century.

Islam

Unlike Christianity, which was brought to Ghana by missionaries who wanted to gain converts, Islam traveled to Ghana along the trade routes. Islam reached northern Ghana around the 15th century, the same time as Christianity was being introduced in the south. Other Muslims came later, from northern Nigeria in the 19th century. They were escaping religious unrest in that country. In the Muslim areas, as in the Christian areas, schools began as religious institutions.

Today, about 16 percent of Ghana's people are Muslims. They follow five basic principles called the Five Pillars of Islam, which form the backbone of the Muslim faith. The first pillar is *shahada*, a statement of faith. Believers declare, "There is no god but God, and Muhammad is his messenger." According to the second pillar, *salat*, Muslims should pray five

A Muslim man prays at a mosque in Tamale during Ramadan.

times a day. The third pillar, *zakat*, says that Muslims should give generously to the poor. The fourth pillar, *sawm*, is fasting, or going without food. Muslims fast during Ramadan, the holiest month of the Muslim calendar. The fifth pillar, *hajj*, is a pilgrimage to Mecca, Saudi Arabia, the holiest city in Islam. If they are physically and financially able, Muslims make a journey to Mecca at least once in their lifetime.

Traditional religions in Ghana are based on the belief that life is a continuous line and that parents and grandparents—all the people who came before—have a strong influence on the lives of people living today. Followers of these traditional religions believe in a supreme figure, or god, known as Nyame in the Akan language and Mawu in the Ewe language.

In traditional Ghanaian religion, people don't worship the supreme god directly because it is too remote. Instead, they communicate through lesser gods who are felt to be a part of the natural world, the world of rivers and trees and mountains.

Members of the Ewe ethnic group paint their faces white and adorn themselves with grasses during a ritual honoring the bush spirit.

Different ethnic groups put more importance on different parts of the natural world. The Asante, for example, see their lesser god in the Tano River. Each area has a local god. Individuals also worship a personal god, one who relates to their own family, community, or household.

In these religions, the spirit world is as real as the people in a person's own family and community. Everyone is linked to the spiritual world through their ancestors. They are a presence in everyday life, and people believe that their ancestors are watching them all the time. They also believe that by living a good life, they can improve the well-being of those who have already died.

Links between people and their ancestors are vital to Ghanaian society.

Sometimes, it is believed, an ancestor will come back to life in order to complete a task that was left undone. The ancestor does this in the form of children, the ancestor's own descendants of a later generation. This is one reason why children are highly valued in Ghanaian society. If a couple has no children, the couple has no one to maintain the link to their ancestors. Some people consider childless couples cursed.

Ghanaians sometimes turn to traditional priests to help them connect to the world of their ancestors and the spirits. Priests also sometimes function as healers. Many people believe that some illnesses have spiritual causes and therefore can be cured by a spiritual person.

A traditional priest performs a ritual in Kumasi.

Rhythms of Life

LIFE IN GHANA IS A RICH MIX OF TRADITIONS. THESE traditions have remained strong even as more and more people move to the cities. Ghanaians still wear traditional fabrics and enjoy music inspired by their ancestors. Ghana's writers use poetry, plays, and fiction to explore their culture in works for readers of all ages. And sports bring people together not just for fun, but to enjoy a feeling of national pride.

Opposite: **Ghanaian children dressed in traditional clothing perform a dance prior to a soccer tournament.**

Young Ghanaians read a newspaper. Poetry, fiction, and journalism are all important to Ghanaian culture.

Rhythms of Ghana

Ghana without music is like a book without words. You need the music to understand the story. Ghanaians sometimes use drums called talking drums to communicate. They make sounds that imitate the Asante language and have long allowed people to pass important messages and news from one village to another. Today, Yacub Tetteh Addy, who was born near Accra, is one of the nation's master drummers. In his hands, a drum becomes a way of speaking.

Drummers demonstrate how to play talking drums at the Manhyia Palace Museum in Kumasi.

A wide variety of drums are used to produce the different tones and rhythms found around the country. The *axatse* is a type of rattle made from a gourd. Beads are attached to the rattle using string, woven like a fishing net. The *gankogui* is a bell or gong made from iron. It is used by the Ewe people to mark the time of the rhythm. People also play various tall, narrow drums, including the *kaganu*, the *kidi*, the *atsimevu*, and the *sogo*.

In southern Ghana, where the Twi language is spoken, drums imitate the tones of the language. A drummer there, using two drums, matches the patterns of the language and can play phrases the local people understand. Each of the drums has a different tone, one high and one low.

Drums and rattles are two of the central elements of traditional Ghanaian music.

In Ghana, dances sometimes tell stories. Here, dancers perform a story about Ghanaian ruler Jerry Rawlings.

Drums are central to creating the music that enables dancers to communicate. In Ghana, dances sometimes tell stories. In one dance, a hungry man disguises himself as a woman in order to enter a market and steal a chicken. Sometimes a dance tells a piece of history. An Ewe dance shows how the Ewe people migrated into the region where they now live. In this dance, the dancers imitate the movements of a bird with their arms. They show how the Ewe followed a bird on their migration from neighboring Benin to Ghana.

Highlife

Ghanaian highlife, a vibrant style of music, began to develop in the 1880s. During colonial times, soldiers from the Caribbean stationed at Cape Coast and Elmina castles brought their European-style brass bands with them. The European and Caribbean influences mixed with traditional African rhythms to form a new style of music: highlife. During World War II, British and American soldiers based in Ghana introduced swing jazz music to the region, and it, too, became part of the mix of this lively musical form. Highlife continues to evolve as each generation brings new ingredients to the music.

Meaning in Cloth

Ghanaians have long created extraordinary patterns in cloth. The Asante people have been making kente cloth since the 12th century. Today, the kente patterns are printed on everything from scarves to umbrellas. When the Asante first made kente, only royalty could wear the cloth. Each pattern was woven for a particular king.

The name *kente* is derived from the word *kenten*, which means "a basket." The patterns originally were woven from the fibers of raffia palm trees, and the cloth looked like a basket. Kente is woven on looms that are 4 inches (10 cm) wide.

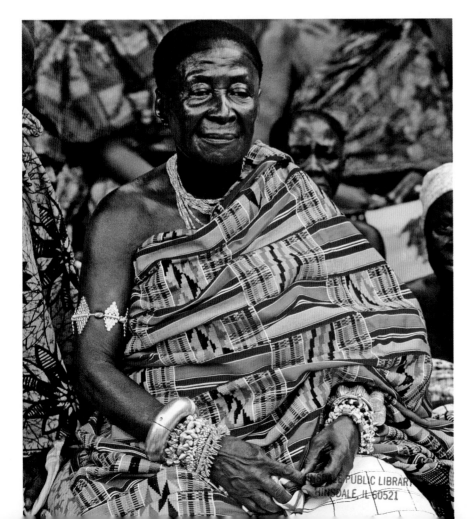

A member of the Asante royal family wears a kente cloth.

The narrow woven strips are sewn together to make fabric. Each pattern is named, usually in reference to events that took place during the reign of an Asante king. These specific patterns represent such qualities as strength, bravery, beauty, valor, and leadership. Brilliant colors—yellow, orange, blue, and red—are mixed in intricate patterns. When the strips are sewn together, they merge into a flowing pattern.

Important kente cloth patterns include *emaa da*, which means "it has not happened before." The Asante king who first saw the pattern was struck by its originality and gave it that name. The *sika futuro* design is created in rich yellow, orange, and red threads. Its name means "gold dust" and refers to the use of gold as money before coins and paper money came into use. This cloth design is considered a symbol of wealth.

A Ghanaian weaves a strip of kente cloth on a handheld loom. Each color has symbolic meaning. For example, yellow represents royalty or wealth.

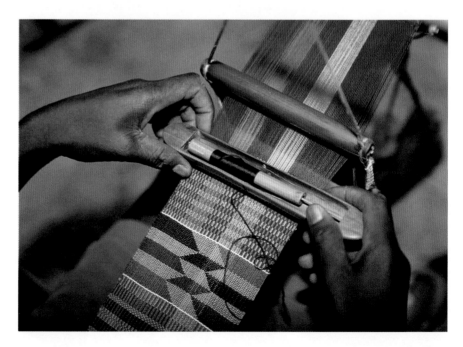

Adinkra cloth, also from the Asante culture, is another fabric that speaks through its patterns. The word *adinkra* means "farewell" and originally was associated with funerals and other rites of passage. The overall pattern of a kente cloth is created to communicate a message, but adinkra cloth is built upon a vocabulary of symbols. More than 80 symbols are used as design elements on a variety of goods made by the Asante. Adinkra symbols represent the thinking, the history, and the beliefs of the Asante people.

The process begins with a solid-color cloth. Designs are carved into a stamping die made from a calabash—a hard-skinned gourd that grows on a vine. The natural dyes that are used come from the bark of the badia tree. The designer first draws squares on the fabric, forming rows, and then stamps the symbols repeatedly in the squares. Because so many different symbols are used, the cloth looks lively.

Each symbol on adinkra cloth represents a different concept.

A man prints symbols on an adinkra cloth.

Some symbols begin with simple shapes such as *akoma*, "the heart." When used as an adinkra symbol, in addition to its usual symbolic meaning of love, akoma also means patience, faithfulness, and endurance. But when the heart is drawn so that the lines are extended into curlicues both inside and out, it has completely different meanings. One is *sankofa*, which means "go back to fetch it." This means that you can learn from the wisdom of the past. By retrieving the past, you can build on it to create a better future. The free-flowing symbol *bi-nka-bi*, which means "do not bite one another," is a symbol of unity. It advises people to avoid fighting.

Keeping Tradition Alive

In the village of Nungua, not far from Accra, children learn to use adinkra symbols on paper they make themselves. They also make their own adinkra stamps. The children, ages 7 to 17, first learn to make the paper from sugarcane leaves. They fashion the paper into greeting cards and small notebooks and decorate them with adinkra symbols. In this way, they keep traditions alive while creating products to sell. With the money they earn, the children buy school supplies and uniforms. Without these, they could not go to school.

The National Theatre

The National Theatre in Accra, built in 1992, hosts all types of performances, including music, dance, and drama. It is home to Ghana's National Dance Company, the National Theatre Players, and the National Symphony Orchestra. It also hosts youth groups such as the Dance Factory and IndigenAfrika.

Ghana has many writers who have explored their own ethnic cultures and experiences in their work. Kwame Anthony Appiah was born in England, raised in Ghana, and now lives in the United States. In his book *In My Father's House*, he discusses how he faces the complex issues of race and culture as an African who lives outside of Ghana. Kofi Awoonor is a poet and novelist. Although he writes in English, he uses his Ewe culture to talk about life in Ghana since independence. His first novel, *This Earth, My Brother: An Allegorical Tale of Africa*, tells the story of a young lawyer trying to understand his newly independent society.

Kwame Anthony Appiah attended college in England and became a philosophy professor. He currently teaches at Princeton University in Princeton, New Jersey.

JOHN F. KENNEDY JR. FOR

Ayi Kwei Armah

FRAGMENTS

a novel

PER
ANKH

Ayi Kwei Armah has written several novels, including *Fragments* (1971). It is the story of a young man who is educated in the United States, returns to Ghana, and finds himself caught between the two worlds.

Ayi Kwei Armah was born to Fante-speaking parents in Takoradi. In books such as *The Beautiful Ones Are Not Yet Born*, he creates stories based on the problems Ghana faced as a former colony. He is especially angry at the way the African history of his people was ignored during his own schooling. "We were brought up to have tiny memories. We were told there was very little history before the white man came. But there is no human group that doesn't have a history."

Bridging Cultures

Playwright and novelist Ama Ata Aidoo was born in 1940, the daughter of a Fante chief. Her plays reflect the struggles of the country, especially after independence, and the sometimes difficult role of women in Ghanaian society.

For many years, Aidoo's writings concerned how many of Ghana's best-educated people had left the country in order to find political freedom and economic opportunity. Once political freedom returned to Ghana, Aidoo began to write about a type of person called a "been-to." A been-to is an educated person who has been to a foreign country and is now back in Ghana, full of new knowledge. This person is a bridge between Ghanaian and Western cultures but often finds that he or she is not at home in either culture. Aidoo's books include *Our Sister Killjoy*, *No Sweetness Here and Other Stories*, and *The Girl Who Can and Other Stories*.

Dozens of writers for adults also write books for children. Many Ghanaian folk stories are retold for children so they can learn more about their own cultures. Among them is a series about a character named Anansi, who is sometimes represented as a spider and sometimes as a man.

Soccer is the national sport of every African country, but in Ghana, soccer is sometimes called a national obsession. Children from toddlers to teenagers play soccer whenever they can find some open space and a ball. Ghanaians are not just enthusiastic about soccer; they are also very good at it. The

Soccer is the most popular sport in Ghana.

Many Ghanaians celebrated when their national team qualified for the 2006 World Cup in Germany.

Ghanaian national team, called the Black Stars, has won the African Cup of Nations three times. In 2006, Ghana qualified to compete in the World Cup, the biggest sporting event in the world of soccer, which takes place every four years.

Soccer Star

One of Ghana's greatest soccer players, Odenke Abbey, was born in 1968 in Accra. Abbey is better known as Marcel Desailly, the name his mother gave him when she married a Frenchman and the family moved to France. Desailly grew up to become a champion on the French national team. In 1998, he helped France win the World Cup. Although Desailly lives in France, he returns to Ghana frequently and still calls it home.

Ghanaians have also been successful in other sports. Ghana has produced many champion boxers, including Ike "Bazooka" Quartey and Alfred "Cobra" Kotey. In 2008, Ghana sent a team of 21 athletes to the Summer Olympic Games, including 7 boxers. All the other team members competed in track-and-field events.

Sprinter Vida Anim (center) was one of 21 Ghanaian athletes who participated in the 2008 Summer Olympics.

A Day
in the Life

In Ghana, the hot climate affects how people go about their daily lives. Long before the sun rises, people are already up, starting their daily work. They try to get as much done as possible before afternoon, when the heat of the day has built up. Farmers head to the fields to do the hard work in the cool morning hours.

Opposite: **A Ghanaian woman prepares a tomato sauce for dinner.**

Workers harvest pineapples on a farm in eastern Ghana. Farming is hot, exhausting work.

Working the Land

Even in Accra and other cities, people have plots of land where they grow food for their families. Both women and men are involved in farming, but they do different tasks. Men generally clear the land and prepare beds for planting. Women plant the crops and carry the water to irrigate them. This often requires carrying heavy cans back and forth over a long distance. Many women carry the water cans balanced on their heads. In some villages, tanks have been set up to collect rainwater for use in homes and on farms.

Women harvest cacao pods. They carry the pods in baskets on their heads.

Women also have to get firewood for their cooking fires. As they use up all the wood around their homes, they must walk farther and farther to get wood. Children often work hard too, carrying water and firewood.

Cooking is time consuming because everything is made by hand. Most people do not have any canned food or flour. Instead, foods are prepared fresh every day. All the while a woman is working, she usually has her youngest child on her back, securely wrapped up in a cloth.

Children collect water from a well. Many Ghanaians rely on wells for drinking water.

Women traders run Makola Market in Accra. They sell food, clothing, household goods, and much more.

To Market They Go

For most women who live along the coast, selling goods at an outdoor market is the main source of family income. Market women, as they are known, have a reputation for being good bargainers. In the bustling markets of Accra and other cities, women are both the salespeople and the shoppers.

At the markets, women sell every item imaginable. They sell imported products, locally made goods, and fresh foods. Makola Market in the center of Accra is a collection of many stalls where people can buy everything from food to clothing to household goods. Bargaining is part of the shopping experience. Prices are not fixed, or printed on signs or tags. Instead, the buyer and seller bargain until they agree on a price.

Go-Slow Traders

Cars and trucks crowd the roads around Accra. Often, traffic hardly moves at all. This gives "go-slow" traders a chance to work. These young men and women walk among the cars that are stuck in traffic, offering a wide variety of goods for sale. They sell everyday goods such as food, cooking pots, and clothing. They also offer very large objects like framed pictures and mirrors.

Close Ties

Family is central to Ghanaian society. In Ghana, aunts, uncles, and cousins are close relatives. When someone moves to the city, that person maintains close ties to their family members who stayed behind. If one family member is sent away to university, that person will later be responsible for the financial well-being of his or her entire extended family.

Family members gather in their village in northern Ghana.

Good Advice

The Akan people, a group that includes the Asante, have many proverbs that reinforce proper behavior. The importance of living a good life, of doing the right thing, is summed up in the proverb, "Disgrace is worse than death." Honoring relatives is clear from the proverb, "If your elders take care of you while you are cutting your teeth, you must in turn take care of them while they are losing theirs." Some proverbs reflect Akan hospitality. One says, "The stranger does not sleep in the street." Others offer practical advice: "If you are in hiding, don't light a fire." And some proverbs are very wise: "There is no medicine to cure hatred" and "No one tests the depth of a river with both feet."

Ghanaian women typically carry their babies strapped to their backs.

In Ghana, showing hospitality is considered part of having a good character—the basis of being a good person. Sharing is also basic to good character. People in Ghana have a duty to take care of their relatives. If relatives show up at your house, you must offer to feed and house them.

Marriage

Entire communities celebrate coming-of-age ceremonies, those moments that mark the transition from one stage of life to the next.

Traditional marriages, known as customary marriages, are at the heart of Ghanaian culture. Even people who get married in a church and have a Western-style wedding often have a customary marriage ceremony first. Family members

A Ghanaian woman wears
a traditional bride's costume.

play a major role in the ceremony. The marriage includes several stages. The engagement ceremony marks the beginning of the couple's marriage. At the ceremony, the groom's family gives the bride's parents valuable gifts, including animals such as cows and sheep. More presents are given to finalize the marriage. The marriage is a contract that creates obligations, duties, and rights between the extended families that will continue throughout their lives.

The Bead Festival

In the village of Odumase-Krobo, an unusual ritual marks the coming-of-age of Dipo girls. The ceremony centers on strands of glass beads, which are made by hand in the village. Powdered glass is placed in a mold of five little cups, colors are added, and the glass is then fired in a kiln. The beads that come out are strung together into long ropes. During the ceremony, which takes place over several days, the girls wear different-colored beads, showing them off proudly.

In the past, girls would be married after the ceremony. Now, a girl is more likely to be attending school when the ceremony takes place. A Dipo woman continues to acquire beads throughout her life. She

inherits some beads from her mother, she buys some herself, and she receives some as gifts from her husband.

An Ancient Game

In Africa, one of the most popular games requires nothing more than some pebbles and a board with 12 or 14 pits in two rows. The game is known by many names throughout Africa: *kikogo, mankala, bao, ayo, nsolo,* and *wari.* In Ghana, it is often called *oware.* In the United States, people know it as *mancala.*

The game begins by placing an equal number of pebbles—or seeds, dried beans, or whatever else is available—in each pit. One player then picks up all the seeds from one pit on his or her side of the board and then drops one pebble into each of the next pits, moving around the board. The second player then does the same. Depending on where the last pebble lands, one player can capture the other player's pebbles. The object of the game is to leave your opponent with no legal move.

Oware boards are often carved wood with figures at one end. Some artisans also carve elegant lids for the boards. But part of the game's appeal is that it can be played anywhere. If players don't have a board, they can dig holes in the ground. The game is several thousand years old. Ancient Ghanaians carved oware boards into stones, and Asante kings played the game on a board made of gold.

Children

Ghanaians consider children a great gift. The average family has about four children. A marriage without children is seen as a curse and usually ends in a separation or divorce.

When a child is born, the baby is kept indoors for the first week. On the eighth day, the baby is brought out to see daylight and to be seen for the first time. The Ga then hold a festive ceremony called an "outdooring." At this time, the baby is given a name. The Akan have a brief ceremony after the birth and then wait longer to name the baby. They do this because they fear that the baby might not survive. If they name the child after an ancestor and then the child dies, it would be a tragedy.

A woman standing in the doorway of her home proudly holds her child.

Fantasy Coffins

In Teshi, a small town near Accra, carpenter Ata Owoo made a coffin in the shape of an eagle for a chief. His work inspired another carpenter, Kane Kwei, to make a special coffin for a relative of his. The business soon took off, and a small industry was born.

Fantasy coffins are made in shapes that reflect the life of the deceased. A taxi driver who drove an old Mercedes-Benz was buried in a smaller, wooden version of the Mercedes. A coffin shaped like a fish celebrated another person's life.

It takes as many as 300 pieces of wood to make a fantasy coffin. Some people order their coffin well in advance of the time they expect to need it, but if a person dies unexpectedly, that is not a problem. In Ghana, funerals often take place weeks or even months after the person's death.

Visitors to Ghana sometimes travel to Teshi to see the fantasy coffins. And many visitors buy small versions of the coffins that they can pack in their suitcases and take home with them as souvenirs.

Ghanaian women on their way to a funeral. In Ghana, events surrounding a funeral often last for a week.

Funerals

Connecting with ancestors is crucial to Ghanaians. People honor the deceased by talking about the life that person lived. Friends and family celebrate the person's life by helping prepare the body for burial.

The body must be bathed and prepared for the next stage, which is seen as a continuation of the life lived on earth. Ghanaians bury the deceased's favorite possessions with the body for use in the next life. People who come to pay their respects often talk to the dead, recalling experiences they had together and wondering how the deceased will be taken care of in the future. As many as 2,000 people may attend a funeral.

A special adinkra cloth is often made for the occasion. The cloth is printed with symbols and sayings. Women wrap the cloth around them to form skirts and turbans and sew it into blouses. Making and wearing the cloth shows respect for the

Red and black are the traditional colors to wear for funerals in Ghana. Funerals are some of the largest and most expensive events in Ghana, much grander than weddings.

deceased. The cloth is often red, a color associated with sad occasions such as the death of a relative. Red is also used in times of war or national crisis, and is one of the colors used in Ghana's national flag.

Eating Well

There is a lively debate among Ghanaians about which food could be called the national dish. One contender is *fufu*, a starchy food made from yams or other root vegetables. To make fufu, the yams are boiled, peeled, and pounded into a sticky mixture. Fufu is quite difficult to make because it thickens and becomes difficult to pound as it cooks. Ghanaians eat fufu as a side dish with a stew made from peanuts.

Vegetable stews are common in Ghana. They include such ingredients as eggplant, tomato, okra, and beans. Corn and plantains, a relative of the banana, are other basic foods in Ghana.

In Ghana, people have many clothing styles to choose from. Some people wear traditional African clothes, and others wear Western-style garments. These choices sometimes send messages.

Kwame Nkrumah, Ghana's first president, often dressed in traditional fabrics and loose-fitting garments to tell his people, "I am an African like you." But former president John Kufuor wore a Western-style suit with a white shirt and tie.

Kwame Nkrumah dressed in traditional Ghanaian clothing when he met the queen of England in 1958.

Kofi Annan wore business suits throughout his career at the United Nations, a place where many people dress in their national costumes. He did this in part because as the UN secretary-general he represented all the people of the world, not just those of his native country.

Women throughout Ghana wear fitted tops made from brightly patterned fabrics. They wrap a matching length of fabric around their lower body. The tops often have puffed sleeves. Most of the traditional clothes women wear are fashioned from locally made fabrics printed with African patterns. In northern Ghana, men wear a smock—a long, loose overshirt or tunic. The loose fit is comfortable for Ghana's hot, dry climate.

Women dressed in adinkra fabric. Many women in rural areas wear traditional clothes.

People in Accra, in southern Ghana, are more likely to wear Western-style clothing than people in the countryside. Businesspeople wear suits, and many men and women wear jeans and casual shirts.

Many women in Ghana braid their hair in intricate patterns. Hair braiders have stalls in the markets. Beautiful painted signs show the variety of hairstyles each hairdresser offers.

Western-style clothes are popular in cities.

Healing the Past

In 1998, Emancipation Day was celebrated for the first time in Ghana. During this weeklong event at the end of July, many people gathered at a former slave fort to mark the end of slavery.

A remarkable part of the event was the reburial of a man named Samuel Carson and a woman named Crystal, two enslaved workers who had died many years before in the United States and Jamaica. Their remains were reburied at Assin Manso, the place where slave traders once decided the value of human beings offered for sale. The president of the National House of Chiefs, Nana Oduro Numapau, presided over the occasion. This chief had traveled to the United States the year before to preside at a ceremony in which he atoned for the Ghanaian chiefs who had taken part in the slave trade.

Celebrations

In Ghana, festivals mark the passage of time. Some festivals celebrate successful hunts. The Aboakyir festival, held on the first Saturday in May, is one such celebration of the hunt. During the event, festivalgoers try to capture a live antelope.

Many villages hold festivals celebrating the harvest of crops, the center of daily life. For instance, the Akan people celebrate the yam harvest.

In August and September, Ga people in Teshi celebrate Homowo, another harvest festival. This colorful festival includes footraces around the village. Children often join in the running. There is no finish line. Instead, it's a continuous race to show happiness for a successful harvest.

National Holidays

January 1	New Year's Day
March 6	Independence Day
March or April	Good Friday
March or April	Easter Monday
May 1	Labor Day
May 25	Africa Day
July 1	Republic Day
December 5	National Farmers' Day
December 25–26	Christmas
December 31	Revolution Day
(varies)	'Id al-Fitr (End of Ramadan)
(varies)	'Id al-Adha (Feast of the Sacrifice)

In Ghana, the struggle to improve daily life continues. Yet the people of Ghana have powerful traditions that they call upon for strength and perseverance.

Ghanaians cheer at a celebration marking the 50th anniversary of their nation's independence.

Timeline

Ghana History

People are living in the region that is **c. 4000** BCE
now Ghana.

The ancient kingdom of Ghana thrives.   **800s** CE

The ancient kingdom of Ghana dies out.   **1000s**

Akan- and Mande-speaking peoples arrive   **1400s**
in what is now Ghana.

Portuguese explorers are the first Europeans   **1471**
to reach Ghana.

The Asante form an empire.   **Late 1600s**

World History

c. 3000 BCE   Forms of writing are invented in China,
India, and Sumeria.

c. 2500 BCE   Egyptians build pyramids in Giza.

c. 563 BCE   The Buddha is born in India.

c. 469 BCE   Socrates is born in Greece.

313 CE   Roman emperor Constantine recognizes
Christianity.

610   The Prophet Muhammad begins
preaching Islam.

618–907   The Tang dynasty rules China.

1206–1227   Genghis Khan rules the Mongol Empire.

1215   King John of England agrees to the
Magna Carta.

1300s   The Renaissance begins in Italy.

1400s   The Inca flourish in the Andes, and the
Aztec thrive in what is now Mexico.

1464   The Songhay Empire is established in
West Africa.

1492   Christopher Columbus arrives in the
Americas.

1502   Enslaved Africans are first brought to the
Americas.

1517   The Protestant Reformation begins.

1776   Americans sign the Declaration of
Independence.

Ghana History

The British declare the Gold Coast a colony.	1874
The Asante come under British rule.	1896
Ghanaians begin fighting for independence.	1947
The Gold Coast gains independence as Ghana.	1957
Construction begins on Akosombo Dam.	1961
The government of Kwame Nkrumah, Ghana's first president, is overthrown.	1966
Prime Minister Kofi Busia is overthrown.	1972
Jerry Rawlings takes power in a military coup.	1979
Rawlings is elected president.	1992
Ghana experiences its first democratic change of power when John A. Kufuor is elected president.	2000
John Atta Mills is elected president.	2008

World History

1804	Haiti becomes independent following the only successful slave uprising in history.
1823	The United States announces the Monroe Doctrine.
1861–1865	American Civil War
1914–1918	World War I
1917	The Bolshevik Revolution brings communism to Russia.
1929	A worldwide economic depression sets in.
1939–1945	World War II
1950s–1960s	African colonies win independence from European nations.
1957–1975	Vietnam War
1989	The cold war ends as communism crumbles in Eastern Europe.
1994	South Africa abolishes apartheid.
2001	Terrorists attack the World Trade Center in New York City and the Pentagon in Arlington, Virginia.
2004	A tsunami in the Indian Ocean destroys coastlines in Africa, India, and Southeast Asia.
2008	The United States elects its first African American president.

Fast Facts

Official name: Republic of Ghana

Capital: Accra

Official language: English

Accra

Ghana's flag

Wli Falls

Official religion:	None
Date of independence:	March 6, 1957
National anthem:	"God Bless Our Homeland Ghana"
Form of government:	Republic
Chief of state:	President
Head of government:	President
Area:	92,456 square miles (239,460 sq km)
Greatest distance north to south:	418 miles (673 km)
Greatest distance east to west:	335 miles (539 km)
Coordinates of geographic center:	8°00' N, 2°00' W
Bordering countries:	Côte d'Ivoire to the west, Burkina Faso to the north, Togo to the east
Highest elevation:	2,887 feet (880 m), Mount Afadjato
Lowest elevation:	Sea level, along the coast
Average high temperatures:	In Accra, 88°F (31°C) in January and 81°F (27°C) in July
Average low temperature:	In Accra, 73°F (23°C) in both January and July
Average annual rainfall:	50 to 83 inches (127 to 211 cm) in the south, 43 to 50 inches (109 to 127 cm) in the north

Elmina Castle

Currency

National population (2008 est.):	23,382,848	
Population of largest cities:	Accra	1,700,000
	Kumasi	650,000
	Tamale	280,000
	Sekondi-Takoradi	270,000

Landmarks:
- ▶ *Centre for National Culture,* Kumasi
- ▶ *Elmina Castle,* Cape Coast
- ▶ *Kakum National Park,* Abrafo
- ▶ *National Theatre,* Accra

Economy: Agriculture is at the heart of Ghana's economy. Cacao is the most important crop. Gold is the leading mining product and the most important source of foreign income. Fishing, especially tuna, and logging also play large roles. Manufactured products include clothing, timber products, aluminum, processed foods, and shea butter. Ghana has improved its communications systems and now is the site of many international call centers. Tourism is a growing industry.

Currency: The Ghanaian new cedi; in 2009, US$1 was equal to 1.34 new cedis.

Weights and measures: Metric system

Literacy rate: 74.8%

Ghanaian children

Common Twi words and phrases:

Wo ho te sen?	How are you?
Me ho ye.	I'm fine.
Mepa wok yew	Please
Meda ase	Thank you
Aane	Yes
Dabi	No

Notable Ghanaians:

Ama Ata Aidoo *Playwright and novelist*	(1940–)
Kofi Annan *Secretary-general of the United Nations*	(1938–)
Kwame Anthony Appiah *Historian and novelist*	(1954–)
Ayi Kwei Armah *Author*	(1939–)
Kwame Nkrumah *First president*	(1909–1972)
Nana Osei Tutu *Asantehene (Asante king)*	(?–1717)

Kofi Annan

To Find Out More

Books

▶ Appiah, Kwame Anthony, and Henry Louis Gates Jr., editors. *Africana: The Encyclopedia of the African and African American Experience*. New York: Basic Civitas Books, 2003.

▶ Cottrell, Anna. *Once upon a Time in Ghana: Traditional Ewe Stories Retold in English*. Leicester, U.K.: Matador Press, 2007.

▶ Salm, Steven J., and Toyin Falola. *Culture and Customs of Ghana*. Westport, Conn.: Greenwood Press, 2002.

Web Sites

▶ **allAfrica.com**
allafrica.com
To keep up with news about Ghana and other African countries.

▶ **Country Profile: Ghana**
news.bbc.co.uk/2/hi/africa/
country_profiles/1023355.stm
For background information on
Ghana from BBC news.

▶ **The World Factbook: Ghana**
www.cia.gov/library/publications/
the-world-factbook/geos/gh.html
For general information about
Ghana, including its economy,
people, and history.

Embassies and Organizations

▶ **Ghana Embassy**
3512 International Dr. NW
Washington, DC 20008
202-686-4520
www.ghanaembassy.org

▶ **Ghana High Commission in Ottawa, Canada**
153 Gilmour Street
Ottawa, Ontario K2P 0N8
www.ghc-ca.com

Index

Page numbers in *italics* indicate illustrations.

A

Abanze, *14*

Abbey, Odenke, 108, *108*

Aboakyir festival, 126

Accra, 13, *13*, 16, 20, 46, 53, *54*,
  55, *61*, 64–65, *64*, *65*, 67, *67*,
  74, 76–77, *79*, 80, 81, *81*, *84*,
  87, 88, 103, *103*, 112, 114, *114*,
  115, 125

Addy, Yacub Tetteh, 96

adinkra cloth, 101–102, *101*, *102*,
  121–122, *124*

adobe bricks, 82

Aetna insurance company, 74

African Americans, 44

African Cup of Nations, 108

agriculture
  Alliance for a Green Revolution in
    Africa, 85
  animal life and, 30
  Asante people, 38
  British colonization and, 68
  cacao, 50, 54, 67, 68–69, *68*, *112*
  cash crops, 69
  climate and, 111
  coastal plains, 17
  crops, 8, 18, 38, 50, 67, 68–69,
    68, 83, *111*, *112*, 122
  economy and, 50, 67, 68, 71
  employment in, 68
  festivals, 126
  forests and, 68
  government and, 53
  irrigation, 112
  livestock, 81, 117
  tropical forests, 18
  urban areas, 112

Agumatsa River, 22

Aidoo, Ama Ata, 106, *106*, 133

Akan language, 38, 64, 80, 91

Akan people, 38, 40, 79, 80, 116,
  119, 126

akoma symbols, 102

Akosombo Dam, 20, 23, 24, *24*,
  54, 76

Akwapim-Togo Ranges, 16, 18

*All God's Children Need Traveling
  Shoes* (Maya Angelou), 44

Alliance for a Green Revolution
  in Africa, 85

Angelou, Maya, 44, *44*

animal life
  baboons, *27*
  birds, 29, 31, 98
  bongo antelope, *26*, 28
  elephants, 28, *28*, 30, 31
  horses, 39
  livestock, 81, 117
  national parks, 27, 28, 31
  poaching, 27
  reserves, *26*, 28, 30
  savannas, 28

Anim, Vida, *109*
Ankobra River, 22
Annan, Kofi, 80, 85, *85*, 124, 133, *133*
Appiah, Kwame Anthony, 104, *104*, 133
Armah, Ayi Kwei, 105, *105*, 133
art, 10, *10*, 12, 83, *83*, 85
Arts Centre, 65, *65*
Asante language, 96
Asante people, 10, 20, 36, 37–38, *37*, 39, *39*, 40, 45, *45*, 46–47, *47*, 48–49, 64, 71, 79, 92, 99, *99*, 100, 101, 116, 118
Asante Uplands, 18
Assin Manso, 126
Atlantic Ocean, 15, 16, 17
Atta, Harruna, 56
Awoonor, Kofi, 104
axatse (musical instrument), 97

B

Baako, Kweku, 56
badia trees, 101
Balme Library, 76
baobab trees, 32, *32*, 33
barracudas, 30, *30*
bauxite mining, 24
"been-to" (traveler), 106
Benin, 24
birds, 29, 31, 98
Birim River, 22
Bismarck, Otto von, 48
black mambas, 29, *29*
Black Stars soccer team, 108, *108*
Black Volta River, 21, 68–69
bongo antelope, *26*, 28
Bonza diamond field, 71
Brim diamond field, 71

British colonization, 9, 24, 38, 44, 45–46, 47, *47*, 48, 49–50, 51, 52, 68
Burkina Faso, 15, 20, 21, 38, 80
Busia, Kofi Abrefa, 54, 55, *55*

C

cacao farming, 50, 54, 67, 68–69, *68*, *112*
calabash (gourd), 101
call centers, 13, *13*
Cape Coast, *15*, 98
Carson, Samuel, 126
carvings, 65, *65*
cedi (currency), 76, *76*
cell phones, 12, *12*, 67
Centre for National Culture, 20
chiefs, 39, 42, 43, 45, 46, 49, 54, 62–63, *63*, 71, 82, 126
Christianity, 87, *87*, 88, *88*, 89
cities. *See also* towns; villages.
    Accra, 13, *13*, 16, 20, 46, 53, *54*, 55, *61*, 64–65, *64*, *65*, 67, *67*, 74, 76–77, 79, 80, 81, *81*, 84, 87, 88, 103, *103*, 112, 114, *114*, 115, 125
    Kumasi, 20, *20*, 39, *45*, 46–47, 48, 49, *72*, 81, 93, 96
    Navrongo Saboro, 82–83
    Sekondi-Takoradi, 17, *17*, 20, *20*, 75, 77, 81
    Tamale, 20, 69, 81, 90
    Tema, 17, 20, 73, 75, *75*
climate, *19*, 22, 25, *25*, 34, 64, 68, 111, 124
clothing, 10, 54, 63, 65, 94, 95, 102, *102*, 114, 115, *117*, 121–122, *122*, 123–125, *123*, *124*, *125*
communications, 10, 12, *12*, 13, *13*, 67, *67*, 95, 96, 98, 101

Convention Peoples' Party (CPP), 51, 53
Côte d'Ivoire, 15, 20, 68, 80
Court of Appeal, 61
crafts, 20, 64-65, *65*, 99–100, *100*, *101*, *102*
Crystal (slave), 126
currency (cedi), 76, *76*

D

Dagomba people, 20
dams, 20, 23, 24, *24*, 54, 76
dance, 94, 98, *98*, 103
Densu River, 22
Dipo people, 118, *118*
Dutch settlers, 44, 46

E

economy
    agriculture, 50, 67, 68, 71
    call centers, 13, *13*, 67
    communications, 67
    exports, 54, 69, 72, 73, 75
    fishing industry, *14*, 20, 73, *73*
    food processing, 69
    manufacturing, 69, 71
    mining, 35, *35*, 59, 67, 70–71, *70*
    service industry, 74–75, *74*
    taxes, 62
    technology and, 66, 67
    timber industry, 27, 34–35, *34*, 45, 67, 69, 72, *72*, 75
    tourism, 74–75
education, 10, 50, 55, 84–85, *84*, 88, 102
electricity, 24, 53, 66, 76–77, *77*
Elmina Castle, 41, *41*, *42*, 44, 46, 74, 98
emaa da pattern, 100

Emancipation Day, 126
English language, 74, 80, 84
European colonization, 9, 24, 38,
    41–42, *41*, 43, 44, 45–46, 47, *47*,
    48, 49–50, 51, 52, 68
Ewe language, 10, 39, 80, 91
Ewe people, 39, 44, 79, 80, *91*, 98
executive branch of government,
    59–60

F

fantasy coffins, 120, *120*
Fante language, 10, 80
Fante people, 39, 45, 46, 63, 73,
    79, 85, *85*, 106, *106*
fishing industry, *14*, 20, 73, *73*
Five Pillars of Islam, 89–90
folk stories, 106
foods, 18, 38, 53, 68, 69, 73, 76, 83,
    90, *110*, 112, 113, 114, 115, 122
Fragments (Ayi Kwei Armah), *105*
fufu (vegetable dish), 122

G

Ga language, 80
gankogui (musical instrument), 97
Ga people, 39, 40, 45, 79, 119, 126
Gbedema, Komla, 51–52
geography
    Akwapim-Togo Ranges, 16, 18
    Asante Uplands, 18
    borders, 15
    coastal plains, 16, 17
    coastline, 15, *15*, 17, *17*, *73*, 75
    elevation, 16, *16*, 18
    high plains, 16, 19
    Kwahu Plateau, 18
    lakes, 16, 20, 23, *23*, 24, 73, 76

land area, 15
Mount Afadjato, 18
rivers, 19, 21–22, *21*, *22*, 23,
    68-69, 76, 80, 92
tropical forests, 16, 18, *18*
Volta Basin, 16, 19
waterfalls, *22*
Ghana Tourist Development
    Company, 85
gold, 38, 40, 42, 45, 48, 67, 70,
    70, 71
Gold Coast, 38, 42, 43, 44, 46, 47,
    50, 51, 52, 64, 80
Golden Stool, 39, 40, *40*, 49
goldweights, 40, *40*, 64
"go-slow" traders, 115
government
    agriculture and, 53
    Britain and, 46, 49, 51, 52, 61
    chiefs, 39, 42, 43, 45, 46, 49,
        54, 62–63, *63*, 71, 82, 126
    common law, 61
    conservation and, 27, 35
    constitution, 54, 59, 60–61
    council of ministers, 59
    council of state, 60
    Court of Appeal, 61
    currency and, 76
    district courts, 61
    elections, 52, 54, 56, 57, *58*,
        59, 60
    electricity and, 76
    executive branch, 59–60
    Fante confederation, 46
    forests and, 27
    Golden Stool, 39, 40, *40*, 49
    governors, 46, 49, 50
    High Court, 61
    independence, 9, *9*, 24, 46, 51,

    52, *52*, 59, *127*
    judicial branch, 59, 60–61, *61*
    kings, 10, 20, 39, 40, 46, 49,
        50, 99, 100, 118, 133
    laws, 51, 60–61, 62, 63
    legislative branch, 59, 60, *60*
    local government, 62
    military, 55, 56, 60
    Parliament, *52*, 56, 60, *60*
    political parties, 53, 54, 57, 60
    presidents, 24, 53, *53*, 54, 55, 56,
        57, *57*, 58, 59, 60, 80, 123,
        123, 133
    "scientific socialism," 53
    Supreme Court, 61
    taxes, 62
    traditional law, 61
Great Britain, 9, 24, 38, 44, 45–46,
    47, *47*, 48, 49–50, 51, 52, 68
Guan people, 79
Guggisberg, Frederick Gordon, 50
Gulf of Guinea, 15, *15*, 21, *73*
Gur language, 80
Gurma people, 79
Gurunsi people, 79

H

harmattan winds, 25
High Court, 61
highlife music, 98
Hill, H. Worsley, 46
historical maps. *See also* maps.
    European Division of Africa
        (1914), *49*
    Gold Coast (1896), *46*
holidays, 126
Homowo festival, 126
hydroelectricity, 53

I

independence, 9, 9, 24, 46, 51, 52, *52*, 59, *127*
India, 51
insect life, 31, *33*, 47, 64
Internet, 67, *67*
Islamic religion, 38, 87, 89–90, *89*, *90*

J

jazz music, 98
judicial branch of government, 59, 60–61, *61*

K

Kakum National Park, 31, *31*
Kejetia Market, 20, *20*
kente cloth, 10, 99–100, *99*, *100*
Kente for the Space Age (Rikki Wemega-Kwawu), 10, *10*
Keta, 44
King, Martin Luther, Jr., 52
kings, 10, 20, 39, 40, 46, 49, *50*, 99, 100, 118, 133
Kitson, Albert, 24
Kotey, Alfred "Cobra," 109
Kufuor, John A., 57, 123–124
Kumasi, 20, *20*, 39, 45, 46–47, 48, 49, *72*, 81, *93*, 96
Kwahu Plateau, 18, 24
Kwa language, 80
Kwame Nkrumah Mausoleum, 64, *64*
Kwei, Kane, 120

L

Lake Bosumtwi, 16, 20
Lake Volta, 16, 23, *23*, 73, 76

languages, 10, 38, 39, 74, 80, 84, 91, 96, 97
Larabanga, 89
legislative branch of government, 59, 60, *60*
Legon, *81*
Leopold, king of Belgium, 48
Limann, Hilla, 56
literature, 44, 95, *95*, 104–106, *104*
livestock, 81, 117
logging industry. *See* timber industry.

M

Makola Market, 65, 114, *114*
malaria, 47
mancala (game), 118, *118*
Mande-Busanga people, 79
Mande people, 38
Manhyia Palace, 20
Manhyia Palace Museum, 96
manufacturing, 69, 71
maps. *See also* historical maps.
    Accra, 65
    geopolitical, *11*
    population density, *82*
    resources, 69
    topographical, *16*
marine life, 30, *30*, 37
markets, 8, 65, *65*, 114, *114*
Mills, John Atta, 57, *57*
mining, 24, 35, *35*, 59, 67, 70–71, *70*
Ministry of Lands, Forestry and Mines, 35
Mole-Dagbon people, 79
Mole National Park, *27*
Mount Afadjato, 16, 18
museums, 20, 64–65, 96

music, 95, 96–98, *96*, *97*, 103
Muslims. *See* Islamic religion.

N

national anthem, 62
national capital, 13, 20, 64–65, *64*, *65*
national flag, 59, *59*
National House of Chiefs, 126
National Museum, 64–65
national parks, 27, *27*, 28, 31, *31*, 74
National Theatre, 103, *103*
Navrongo Cathedral, 86
Navrongo Saboro, 82–83
New Patriotic Party (NPP), 57
Nixon, Richard, 52
Nkrumah, Kwame, 24, 51–52, 53–55, *53*, *54*, 80, 123, *123*, 133
Northern Territories, 49
Numapau, Nana Oduro, 126
Nungua, 102

O

Obruni Wa Wu Market, 65
Obuasi gold mine, 70, *70*
Odumase-Krobo, 118, *118*
Olympic Games, 109, *109*
opencast mining, 70
Osei Tutu, Nana, 39, 40
oware (game), 118, *118*
Owoo, Ata, 120

P

palm oil, 45
Parliament, 60, *60*
people
    ages of, 79
    Akan, 38, 40, 79, 80, 116, 119, 126

ancestors, 92–93, *92*, 95, 119, 121
Asante, 10, 20, *36*, 37–38, *37*, *39*, *39*, 40, 45, *45*, 46–47, *47*, 48–49, 64, 71, 79, 92, 99, *99*, 100, 101, 116, 118
"been-to" (traveler), 106
chiefs, 39, 42, 43, 45, 46, 49, 54, 62–63, *63*, 71, 82, 126
children, 93, 94, 119, *119*
climate and, 111, 124
clothing, 10, 54, *63*, 65, *94*, 95, 102, *102*, 114, 115, *117*, 121–122, *122*, 123–125, *123*, *124*, *125*
coming-of-age ceremonies, 116, 118, *118*
crops, 126
Dagomba, 20
Dipo, 118, *118*
diseases, 47
early people, 37
education, 10, 50, 55, 84–85, *84*, 88, 102
employment, 13, *13*, 24, 66, 67, 68, 74, *111*
Ewe, 39, 44, 79, 80, *91*, 98
families, 39, *63*, 73, 85, 92, *92*, 112, 114, 115, *115*, 116–117, 119, 121
Fante, 39, 45, 46, *63*, 73, 79, 85, *85*, 106, *106*

food, 18, 38, 53, 68, 69, 73, 76, 83, 90, *110*, 112, 113, 114, 115, 122
funerals, 120, 121–122, *121*, *122*
Ga, 39, 40, 45, 79, 119, 126
"go-slow" traders, 115
Guan, 79
Gurma, 79
Gurunsi, 79
hair, 125
health care, *74*, 93
hospitality of, 116
housing, 37, *37*, 81, *81*, 82–83, *83*
languages, 10, 38, 39, 74, 80, 84, 91, 96, 97
Mande, 38
Mande-Busanga, 79
marriage, 116–117, *117*, 118
military service, 60
Mole-Dagbon, 79
names, 80, 119
"outdooring" ceremony, 119
population, 20, 22, 64, *82*
rural areas, 82–83
slavery, 42, *42*, 43, *43*, 44, 71, 126
Soninke, 38
urban areas, *81*
voting rights, 60
water, 112, 113, *113*
women, 43, 54, 58, 69, 71, 73, 74, 82, 83, *83*, 106, *110*, 112, *112*, 113, 114, *114*, *116*, *119*, 121, *121*, 124, *124*, 125

phone cards, 10, *10*, 12
plant life
    badia trees, 101
    baobab trees, 32, *32*, 33
    calabash, 101
    conservation, 35, *35*
    forests, *18*, 31, *31*, 34, *34*, 35
    savannas, 19, 28, 33
    scrub, 33
    skywalks and, 31, *31*
    tropical forests, 18, *18*, 31, *31*
    Volta Basin, 19, *19*
population, 20, 22, 64, 82
port cities, 17, *17*, 20, 75
Portuguese traders, 41–42, *41*, 44
Pra River, 22
Prempeh I (Asante king), 49, *50*
Prempeh, Nana Osei Agyeman, 49

Q
Quartey, Ike "Bazooka," 109

R
railroads, 50
Rawlings, Jerry, 56, *56*, 57, 98
religion
    ancestors and, 92–93
    Christianity, 87, *87*, 88, *88*, 89
    education and, 88
    Five Pillars of Islam, 89–90
    health care and, 93

Islamic, 38, 87, 89–90, *89, 90*
missionaries, 88, 89
mosques, 89, *90*
Navrongo Cathedral, 86
priests, 40, 93, *93*
Ramadan (Islamic holy
     month), 90
traditional beliefs, 87, 91–93, *93*
reptilian life, 28, 29, *29*
roadways, *27*, 50, 115

S

Sekondi-Takoradi, 17, *17*, 20, *20*, 75,
     77, 81
service industry, 74–75, *74*
shea butter, 69
shipping industry, 75, *75*
skywalks, 31, *31*
slave trade, 42, *42*, 43, *43*, 44,
     71, 126
soccer, 94, 107–108, *107, 108*
Soninke people, 38
sports, 94, 107–109, *107, 108, 109*
St. Augustine's College, 10
Supreme Court, 61

T

Takoradi. *See* Sekondi-Takoradi.
talking drums, 96, *96*
Tamale, 20, 69, 81, *90*
Tano River, 22

Tema, 17, 20, 73, 75, *75*
Teshi, 120, 126
timber industry, 27, 34–35,
     34, 35, 45, 67, 69, 72,
     72, 75
Timber Nkwanta, 77
Togo, 15, 20, 24, 80
tourism, 44, 74–75, 120
towns. *See also* cities; villages.
     Keta, 44
     Teshi, 120, 126
trading beads, 71
transportation, 17, *17, 21*, 75, *75*
tropical forests, 16, 18, *18*
tro-tro (minivan), 75, *75*
Tutu, Asantehene Osei, 20
Tutu, Nana Osei, 133
Twi language, 80, 97

U

United Nations (UN), 85, 124
United Party, 54
University College, 50
University of Cape Coast, 55
University of Ghana, 76, 77, *77*, 85

V

Valco Aluminum, 77
villages. *See also* cities; towns.
     Abanze, *14*
     electricity in, 77

families in, *115*
festivals, 126
Larabanga, 89
Nungua, 102
Odumase-Krobo, 118, *118*
Timber Nkwanta, 77
Volta Basin, 16, 19
Volta River, 19, 21, *21*, 23, 76, 80

W

water, 19, 22, 28, 34, 50, 76, 77, 82,
     112, 113, *113*
waterfalls, 22
weaving, 99–100, *100*
Wemega-Kwawu, Rikki, 9–10, 13
White Volta River, 21
wildlife. *See* animal life; insect
     life; marine life; plant life;
     reptilian life.
Wli Falls, *22*
women, 43, 54, 58, 69, 71, 73,
     74, 82, 83, *83*, 106, *110*,
     112, *112*, 113, 114, *114*,
     116, 119, 121, *121*, 124,
     124, 125
World Cup soccer tournament,
     108, *108*
World War II, 51, 98

Y

al-Ya'qubi (Arab writer), 38

Meet the Authors

Jason Lauré has been photographing Africa since the 1970s and considers Ghana one of his favorite places to work. He admires the energy and ingenuity of the Ghanaian people. His most recent visit to a data processing center in Accra showed him how quickly Ghana has entered the modern electronic age. On a recent trip, he also had a close-up view of the

beauty of Ghana's forests when he took a walk on the Kakum skywalk.

Mr. Lauré was born in Chehalis, Washington, and attended Columbia University in New York City before working for the *New York Times*. He has written more than a dozen books in the Enchantment of the World series with his partner, Ettagale Blauer.

Ms. Blauer has traveled across Africa with Mr. Lauré, learning about many cultures and gathering material for the books they have written together. They have crossed the Sahara, been through the gold and diamond mines of southern Africa, and explored the jungles of central Africa. During her travels, Ms. Blauer came to particularly appreciate Ghanaian culture. She respects the way Ghanaians combine traditional ways with an ability to use modern technology to better their lives. She also admires Ghana's beautiful kente cloth and the design and artisanship found in the gold objects that are central to Asante culture.

In addition to her writings for young people, Ms. Blauer is the author of *African Elegance*, a book that explores the crafts and cultures of sub-Saharan Africa. Ms. Blauer was born in New York City and graduated from Hunter College.

Photo Credits